CAN YOU BELIEVE YOUR EYES?

CAN YOU BELIEVE YOUR EYES ?

OVER 250 ILLUSIONS AND OTHER VISUAL ODDITIES

J.R. Block
HOFSTRA UNIVERSITY

Harold E. Yuker
HOFSTRA UNIVERSITY

GARDNER PRESS, INC.
NEW YORK • LONDON • SYDNEY

Library of Congress Cataloging-in-Publication Data

Block, J. R.
   Can you believe your eyes? : over 250 illusions
and other visual oddities / J.R. Block, Harold E.
Yuker.
         p.   cm.
      Bibliography: p.
      Includes index.
      Summary: Presents over 250 visual illusions
gathered from around the world to explore the
psychology of vision. Discusses the phenomenon
of human perception and the use of illusions in
society.
      ISBN 0-89876-163-8 : $19.95
      1. Optical illusions.   2.Visual perception.
[1. Optical illusions. 2. Visual perception] I. Yuker,
   Harold E. II. Title.
   QP495.B56   1989
   152.14'8—dc20   89-11950
                                           CIP
                                            AC

10 9 8 7 6

Book Design by Sidney Solomon and Paul Agule
Page mechanicals by Russell Bianca
Typesetting by Smith, Inc.
Printing and binding by Hamilton Printing Co.

This book is dedicated to
Patricia Block,
a wife to one of us,
a friend to both of us,
and to
Hofstra University,
a home for all three of us

CONTENTS

1. INTRODUCTION **9**

2. AMBIGUOUS FIGURES **15**

3. UNSTABLE FIGURES **31**

4. FIGURE-GROUND ILLUSIONS AND CAMOUFLAGE **37**

5. ILLUSORY FIGURES **51**

6. VISUAL AFTEREFFECTS **65**

7. APPARENT MOVEMENT AND SUBJECTIVE COLOR **77**

8. IMPOSSIBLE FIGURES **87**

9. SHAPE DISTORTION **99**

10. SIZE DISTORTION **113**

11. LENGTH DISTORTION **123**

12. CONSTANCY **137**

13. DISTANCE ESTIMATION AND DEPTH PERCEPTION **147**

14. VISUAL ATTENTION AND ORGANIZATION **161**

15. PERCEPTUAL SET **173**

16. WORD PERCEPTION **183**

17. STANDING ON YOUR HEAD MAKES A DIFFERENCE **189**

18. TWO EYES ARE BETTER THAN ONE **215**

19. OTHER ILLUSIONS **223**

20. EPILOGUE **237**

REFERENCES **241**

COPYRIGHT ACKNOWLEDGEMENTS **245**

OTHER WORKS BY THE AUTHOR **249**

We wish to express our deep appreciation to Robert Noble, the retired Secretary of Hofstra University, and to Jack Ruegamer, Director of Printing and Publications at Hofstra University. Each was invaluable in assisting us to produce the two decks of illusions playing cards which represented the beginning of this book.

Additionally, we want to thank Professor Donald R. Booth, Chairperson of the Department of Fine Arts at Hofstra University, and two of his undergraduate Fine Arts majors, Evangelos Gianakos and Karen Thomas for their assistance in preparing much of the final art work for this book.

CHAPTER 1

INTRODUCTION

This is a book which requires you to participate in more ways than simply reading. To really enjoy it you will have to do a great many things with it that you don't do with other books.

For example, when you get to Chapter 17, you will be constantly turning the book upside down and then right side up to see what is there. In some cases, you will have to turn the book left or right to see the effect.

There are several chapters where you will have to use a ruler to convince yourself that what you see is really not true (Chapters 9, 10 and 11).

In Chapter 6, you cannot simply look at the illustrations to see the illusions. You must stare at them for approximately 30 seconds. Even then, to see the illusion you do not look at the book. You must shift your gaze to a blank sheet of paper, or the wall, or some other blank space to see the effect.

For most of Chapter 18 you have to cross your eyes to see the illusions.

You have to move away from the book to see two illusions (5.18 and 5.19) but, you have to put the book practically up against your nose to see two others (19.15 and 19.16).

To see several of the illusions, you will have to xerox the illustration, paste it on a piece of cardboard, and then spin it on the end of a paper clip (6.8, 6.9, 7.6, 7.7 and 7.8). There is another which you can only see by looking at it through a pin hole.

You have to wiggle the book slightly to see several illusions (7.1, 7.2, 19.8, 19.9 and 19.10), while for others you will have to tilt the book away from you so that it is almost horizontal, and look at them from the edge of the page (12.8, 12.9 and 18.9).

Several of the visual oddities we have included in Chapter 16 deal with words. To be appreciated, they will have to be read aloud.

Some of the illusions included here are "one-time" illusions. That is, once you have seen them, the novelty is gone. Indeed, in many cases, whatever you thought you saw before the visual principle was made known to you, will never be seen again! In these illustrations the pleasure you will experience after that lies in showing it to others. Other illusions are perpetual. That is, although you know your perception is incorrect, you will still be unable to change it! In that sense, this is a book you will be able to go back to over and over again for years to come.

This book doesn't really have a beginning, a middle, or an end. With few exceptions each chapter can stand on its own, and even each illustration can be enjoyed separately from the others. You can start anywhere and go either forward or backward.

Basically this book is about vision. Vision is one of our most important means of getting information from the world around us. But what is vision? It is a process that involves the reception of *electromagnetic energy* by the eyes. This kind of energy travels in waves, which vary greatly in length. Some electro-magnetic waves, called gamma waves, are extremely short, measuring only about 4 ten-trillionths of an inch in length! In contrast, some are over 18 miles long! These are the electro-magnetic waves used for trans-oceanic broadcasts. In between are the wave lengths used for X-rays, infra-red radiation, short wave and regular broadcast radio signals.

The wave lengths your eyes receive make up what is called *the visible spectrum*. They are relatively short waves, somewhat longer than X-rays. They range from 16 millionths of an inch to about 32 millionths of an inch in length. Receptors in the eye are sensitive to this band of radiation, much as radio tuners are sensitive to wave lengths of the same kind of energy, but of lengths of from about a tenth of a mile to a third of a mile.

Sensation results when this energy is received by the eye and transmitted to the brain. The receptors in the eyes, called *rods* and *cones*, convert the energy into nerve impulses and send it on to the brain. The brain connects these impulses with other brain processes to make them meaningful. This is called *perception*. This book is about visual perception—the interpretation of the visible spectrum.

The book is not intended to be scholarly. Though there are occasional explanations of visual principles, they are not presented in great detail. There are several reasons for this. First, we wanted the book to have a broad range of appeal, from professionals to laypersons. Second, many principles underlying the illustrations here are not understood even today, although as you will see, many of the illusions in this book have been around for over a century, and a few are thousands of years old! Finally, where explanations are available, they often are very complex and require specialized knowledge.

The book focuses on many pleasurable and interesting aspects of vision. We have tried to concentrate on those visual principles we think people will find most intriguing rather than to attempt balanced coverage. We present a wide range of examples of visual principles, but focus most on illusions.

Illusions are misperceptions. They are interpretations of stimuli that do not follow from the sensations received by the eye. When we witness an illusion, we perceive something that does not correspond to what is actually out there—what exists in the real world. Illusions fool us; they convince us of things that are not true. The interesting thing is we seem to enjoy being fooled in this way!

Magicians use illusions all the time. In fact, magicians are sometimes referred to as illusionists. Famous magicians, like the great Harry Houdini, admit that what they do is create illusions. They do not do the impossible, they just seem to do it.

Illusions are different from both hallucinations and delusions. Illusions are misperceptions that are perceived by most people, and that are based on a specific stimulus viewed under certain conditions. Some experiments with animals indicate that several species of mammals and birds are "fooled" by illusions in much the same way we are. Not all human beings are fooled by illusions. For example, persons who come from cultures in which there are few straight lines and angles would not be fooled by several of the illusions in this book.

Hallucinations are usually seen by only one individual. Most often they are experienced by people who suffer from specific kinds of mental illness, or who are influenced by drugs or extreme amounts of alcohol. Hallucinations are false perceptions that occur in the *absence* of appropriate external stimuli, whereas illusions are misinterpretations of external stimuli that are, in fact, present.

Although we shall discuss and illustrate visual illusions, illusions and hallucinations can involve any of our senses—sight, sound, touch, taste, or smell.

Delusions are different from both illusions and hallucinations. They are beliefs, not perceptions. Like hallucinations, they tend to be found in people who are mentally ill. A person may have delusions of grandeur (believing that he or she is a very important person) or delusions of persecution (believing someone or something is out to harm him or her), when the facts clearly do not support these beliefs.

Many common perceptions involve illusions although most people are not aware of it. That is, much of what we perceive does not correspond to the stimulation of our sense organs. Thus, for example, we do not see a person who is walking away from us as getting smaller and smaller, even though the image in our eyes rapidly decreases in size. Yet anthropologists have described tribes that are greatly puzzled by this phenomenon when they first perceive it.

We also get illusions of depth in paintings, 3-D movies, stereopticons, and holographs, even though these are presented to us on two-dimensional surfaces.

The "moon illusion" discussed in Chapter 10 is a familiar natural illusion. The moon illusion refers to the fact that when the moon is on the horizon it appears to be quite large, but when it is overhead, it seems very much smaller. Philosophers and scientists have been trying to explain this since Ptolemy, an astronomer who lived in Alexandria in the second century.

One very powerful illusion is called the size-weight illusion. However, since it involves the use of containers, we cannot present it in this book. We can describe it, though, and you can demonstrate it for yourself and your friends.

Take a small attache case, a small over-night bag, and a large three-suiter suitcase, and fill the attache case with some heavy material such as books. After you have determined its weight, put books of the same weight in the over-night case and the three-suiter. Ask someone to lift each case and tell you which is the heaviest. We virtually guarantee that the attache case will be judged to be *much* heavier than the others, even though they all weigh exactly the same.

In part this is explained by our expectations. When we see the large case, we prepare our muscles to lift something heavy. When it is only filled to a portion of its capacity, it goes up easily. On the other hand, we don't expect to have a particularly difficult time lifting the small attache case, and we are suprised by the weight.

You can get the same effect using food containers. For example, you can use cans holding 8 ounces, 16 ounces, and 32 ounces of material. Put dirt or pebbles into each can so that all three are exactly the same weight, and cover them with tin foil. Most people will swear that the smallest weighs the most, and the largest the least. Even though you prepared them yourself, you too may have difficulty accepting that they are all the same weight!

Perception may also be distorted in other ways. One such distortion results from what is called *selective perception*. Selective perception is a result of the influence of personal factors on perception. What a person perceives reflects that person's past learning and present state of mind, as well as what is actually "out there." A Republican and a Democrat who listen to the same political speech will "hear" and remember different things. If you ask them about it afterwards, it may be hard to believe they listened to the same speech.

Being aware of these various types of perceptual distortions should make people less willing to believe their eyes—or any of their other senses. What you perceive does not always correspond to reality.

Optical illusions are related to the way the brain processes incoming information. As the brain receives impulses from the eye, it tries to make the information meaningful. Factors such as prior learning, and the total visual context, in addition to the object upon which we focus, and the extent to which we are prepared to receive specific information, all play important roles in interpretation.

The process usually involves two steps. First, drawing attention to an object, and second, making it meaningful. This book presents examples of these factors, many of which are very useful in such fields as advertising, art, fashion design, equipment design, and stage design. In fact, some of the basic principles go beyond vision. Some relate to hearing, and others to social behavior.

However, most of the book deals with the misperceptions called illusions. Although we have included over 250 illustrations, this is not an exhaustive presentation. Many illusions have not been included here. Some, such as the size-weight illusion described earlier, require equipment which goes beyond the limits of the printed page. Other illusions are not visual. They may involve hearing, the sense of touch, or other nonvisual sensations.

As we stated earlier, not all illusions are universal. There may be some that you or your friends do not see, or some that one person sees, but another does not. There is no simple explanation for this variability in perception. Nonetheless, there are enough illustrations that we believe you will find many hours of pleasure in going through these pages.

CHAPTER 2

AMBIGUOUS FIGURES

The first set of illustrations we present is among those that are perpetual. Once you see them they will persist forever. In each drawing in this chapter there are at least two different figures. You may not see both initially. Therefore, we will provide cues for you to differentiate one from the other. Once you see each separate figure, you should have no difficulty in seeing both—or, in one case, all three.

Some people, on first exposure, apparently see only one of the two or more figures. They may require additional cues to see the others. The fascinating aspect of ambiguous figures is that once one sees both pictures, it is impossible to focus on only one without the other "popping" into your vision from time to time! When you have made meaning out of the different forms, you will find that both illustrations are equally good, and that neither dominates the other. This illustrates the importance of learning in perception.

On the other hand, even when you know that two pictures are there, you cannot see them both at the same time!

**Figure 2.1 – An eskimo?
An Indian head?**

Figure 2.1 is called the *Wilson* figure. It is both an Eskimo and an Indian head at the same time. The dark area on the right represents the opening of an igloo with an Eskimo facing inward. Alternatively, the dark area can be seen as an Indian's headdress. The Indian's ear is the Eskimo's arm, and the Eskimo's legs are the Indian's neck.

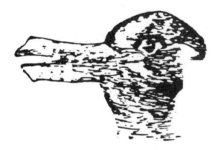

**Figure 2.2 – A rabbit?
A duck?**

Figure 2.2 can be seen as either a rabbit or a duck depending on whether you see it as facing right or left. The duck's bill becomes the rabbit's ears. This figure was developed by a psychologist named Joseph Jastrow about 1900.

The bird in Figure 2.3 can be seen as either a goose or a hawk depending on the direction in which we assume it to be flying. The long neck of the goose flying toward our left becomes the tail of the hawk.

Figure 2.3 – Is this a goose or a hawk?

Figure 2.4 — Seal or donkey?

A number of similar two-ended ambiguous figures are presented in Figure 2.4, 2.5, and 2.6 (Fisher, 1968a).

Figure 2.4 is either a seal or a donkey's head. The seal's flippers, which are in the air, also serve as the donkey's ears. The donkey's nostrils are the seal's eyes.

Figure 2.5 — Duck or squirrel?

Figure 2.5 is either a duck coming toward you, or a squirrel seen from the rear. The duck's tail feathers are the squirrel's head, while the duck's head is the squirrel's tail.

Figure 2.6 — Rabbit or Indian?

Figure 2.6 is either a rabbit or the back of an Indian's head. The rabbit's head and ears form the band and single feather at the back of the Indian's head.

Figure 2.7 — Husband and father-in-law.

In 1961 a figure called "Husband and father-in-law" was published and is presented as Figure 2.7 (Botwinick, 1981). The old man is seen in profile with the dark areas representing a coat pulled up close to his jaw line. His nose is the tip of the young man's chin as the latter is looking away from you. The nearly straight horizontal line near the middle of the picture serves as the old man's mouth, or a neck band for the young man.

Figure 2.8 — A young woman? An old woman?

Do you see an old woman or a young one in Figure 2.8? Both are there. Think of the tip of the old woman's nose as the young woman's chin, or vice versa. The old woman is seen in full profile while the young woman is turned away from you in about one-quarter profile. The illusion was first published in *Puck* in 1915 and was entitled "My wife and my mother-in-law" (Hill, 1915).

In 1968 another psychologist developed an ambiguous figure with three faces using much the same technique. He called it "Mother, father and daughter" (Fisher, 1968b). Near the middle of the figure is a small dark spot, which serves as the eye of the father. He is facing the right edge of the page. He has a large nose and a drooping mustache.

The spot that serves as the eye for the father is also the mother's left eye. She is facing the left edge of the page. She has a short, thin lipped mouth, and a large nose. The tip of her nose is the tip of the daughter's chin. The daughter also faces left and has a very small nose, the top of which is missing in the drawing. The spot which represents her parents' eyes is her ear, and her father's nose becomes hair hanging down the back of her neck.

Figure 2.9 — Mother, father and daughter.

Still another ambiguous figure is shown in Figure 2.10 (Bugelski & Alampay, 1961). It can be seen as either a man's face or a rat. The two, small round areas near the top left are either the rat's ears or the man's glasses. The man's nose is the rat's head, and his chin the rat's tail.

Figure 2.10 — Man or rat?

If people are shown pictures of animals before seeing Figure 2.10 they will be predisposed to see the rat.

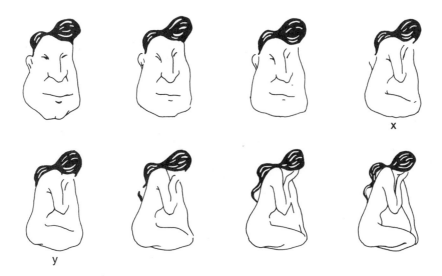

Figure 2.11 – Developing an ambiguous figure.

Figure 2.11 shows the development of an ambiguous figure by progressive modification of an image. In this drawing, the figures marked "X" and "Y" are identical. If you showed the top row to someone, and covered the bottom row, the person would have difficulty seeing the girl in the figure marked "X." Conversely, if you covered the top row, the person would find it hard to see the man's face in the image marked "Y." This illustrates the influence of expectations on perception (Fisher, 1967b).

You can also see the role of expectation in Figure 2.12. If you are led to believe the figure is an advertisement for a costume ball, you can see a man with a woman who is wearing a long gown. The man seems to be carrying a handkerchief, and the woman, whose features are not visible, is wearing a large bonnet.

However, suppose you are told that the poster is for a trained seal act. Now the part of the illustration which was perceived as a woman becomes a seal balancing a ball on its nose, and the handkerchief is seen as a fish! (From Benjamin, Hopkins, & Nation, 1987)

**Figure 2.12 – Come to the costume ball.
See the trained seal!**

Figure 2.13 — Man, or woman and baby?

Another ambiguous figure which uses the human face to form a different picture is Figure 2.13 (Fisher, 1967a). It can be seen as a man's face in profile, or a woman holding a baby. The woman's face is small and round. She has long blond hair which serves as the man's nose, and her face is the man's eye. Her arm is the man's chin line, and the baby's face can be seen as the man's ear just under the striped area on the left of the figure.

Figure 2.14 — The Boys from Syracuse.

The well-known caricaturist Al Hirshfeld designed the ambiguous figure in Figure 2.14 to promote the musical "The Boys from Syracuse." This appeared in the Drama Section of *The New York Times* on the 29th of September, 1963. Hirshfeld was able to draw the two faces, one looking left, the other looking right, in a single face so that from time to time as you look at the picture, one boy seems to be in front of the other, and then they seem to change places (Kolers, 1964).

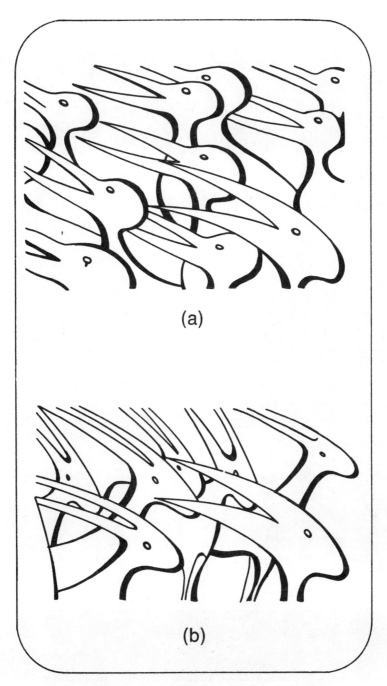

(a)

(b)

Figure 2.15 — Is the figure in the lower right of each picture a bird or an antelope?

Figure 2.15 shows the importance of context in ambiguous figures. The lower right-hand figure in each group is the same but can be seen as either a bird or an antelope depending on the context in which it is seen (From Hanson, 1958).

Figure 2.16 – Two faces? A vase?

Since there is no clear figure or background in Figure 2.16, you can see it as either a vase, or as two faces. Once again, since neither figure is "better" than the other, the two images "pop" in and out of our perception. This illustration was first published in about 1915.

Figure 2.17 —

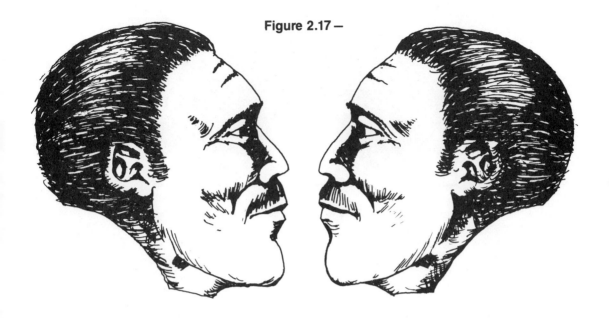

Figure 2.18 —

Later in this book we will talk about the importance of expectation in determining what we perceive. Under normal conditions, it is not possible to predict whether a person will see faces or the vase first. However, if you were to show someone the two profiles in Figure 2.17 before seeing 2.16 they will see faces first. If they are shown 2.18 first, 2.16 will be seen as a vase.

Figure 2.19 — Lovers or a mosque?

In Figure 2.19 we have tilted the two heads so that the foreheads are touching. With a little imagination you can see a mosque-like structure of the kind one would associate with Middleastern houses of worship. Once both the lovers and the mosque are perceived, one's attention alternates between the two.

Figure 2.20 — Faces or a Candle?

A variation of the lovers can be seen here. Figure 2.20 can be seen as two faces or a lit candle. (From Kettlekamp, 1974).

Figure 2.21 — The Canadian flag — two angry men?

A similar effect can be seen in the Canadian flag, but in this case the two faces are not lovers, but can be interpreted as two angry men. If you look at the upper left- and right-hand edges of the maple leaf, the leaf itself can be seen as separating two angry faces with long noses, and their foreheads pressed together much as in Figure 2.19. The faces can be seen just above an imaginary line between the extreme points on the leaf just above the base looking into the center. In Canada they are called Jack and Jacques. Perhaps they are arguing about the merits of English vs. French.

Figure 2.22 — Slave Market with the Apparition of the Invisible Bust of Voltaire (Dali).

Ambiguous figures have been used by well-known artists as well. Figure 2.22 is a painting by Salvador Dali, called *Slave Market with the Apparition of the Invisible Bust of Voltaire*. Voltaire's bust is made up primarily of the large white area slightly to the left of the center of the picture. His eyes are also the faces of two nuns, and his cheeks are their white collars. Once you see both the nuns and the bust of Voltaire, the images will alternate (Atkinson, et al., 1987).

Figure 2.23 — Scott Kim.

Figure 2.23 presents a novel unstable figure in the form of a person's name. This design was developed by a calligrapher in the United States by the name of Scott Kim. He designed the letters in both his first and second name so you can read the figure as either name—and each will alternately appear in your consciousness! (From *Omni*, November, 1988)

Figure 2.24 — All is Vanity.

A similar effect had been created earlier by an unknown artist at the turn of the century. It is called *All is Vanity*. It can either be seen as a young woman seated at a vanity table looking in the mirror, or as a skull.

CHAPTER 3

UNSTABLE FIGURES

This chapter also contains perpetual illusions. However, the illusion here lies in the contradictory cues for depth perception which make it very difficult to determine what part of the given figure is closest to you. Look once and one side seems closer—but look again, and the other side seems closer!

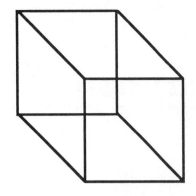

Figure 3.1 — A reversible figure.

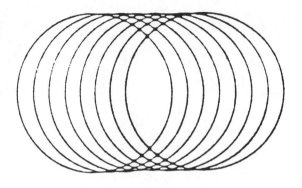

Figure 3.2 — Is the top or bottom circle closest?

In Figure 3.1, a cube is seen, but it is unclear which corner is closest. As a result, the figure seems to pop in and out. This is called the *Necker Cube*. In Figure 3.2, the same is true for a series of overlapping circles.

Figure 3.3 again contains contradictory cues to depth perception. You are not sure which edge, of what could be tail feathers of an arrow, is closest to you. As a result, the figure becomes unstable.

Similarly in Figure 3.4, the white diamond areas alternately "pop" in and out such that either the top right or bottom left can be seen as closer to you. This figure is known as *Thiery's Figure*.

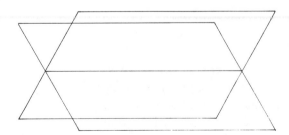

Figure 3.3 — Are the short fins near or far?

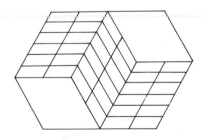

Figure 3.4 — Does this figure "pop" in and out?

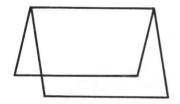

Figure 3.5 – Can you focus on the design in the figure above?

Unstable figures can be extremely simple and familiar forms such as in Figure 3.5, which could be a folded piece of paper, or fairly complex and unfamiliar ones such as the one in Figure 3.6.

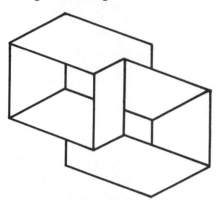

Figure 3.6 – Can you focus on the design in the figure above?

In the case of 3.5, the lowest of the horizontal lines sometimes seems to be closer than the middle one, and sometimes further away. In 3.6, the small diamond-shaped figures seem to be a hollow center of larger figures. These larger figures seem to change their direction from moment to moment.

Figure 3.7 – Six cubes? Seven cubes?

In Figure 3.7, you can see either six or seven cubes depending upon whether you see the black diamond shapes as the tops or bottoms of the cubes.

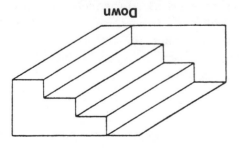

Figure 3.8 – Down

In Figure 3.8, one can see a staircase with a wall behind it. The figure is equally good from either side, it appears right side up even when turned upside down. This is known as *Schroeder's staircase*.

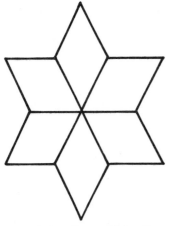

Figure 3.9 — Does this figure appear three- dimensional?

Figure 3.9 is unstable in several ways. First, it can be seen as a flat six-pointed figure made up of diamond shapes. Next, it can be seen as an equilateral triangle figure overlaid with three diamond shapes. Finally, if you stare at it for about 30 seconds, it will seem to take on interesting three-dimensional shapes with the diamond shapes popping inward and outward.

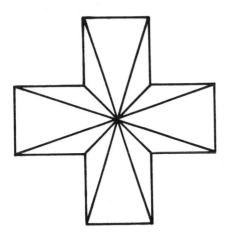

Figure 3.10 — This figure seems to change shapes.

A similar effect can be seen in Figure 3.10. It appears to be a cross which has been divided into various triangles. As you stare at it, the smaller triangles sometimes appear to be folds in a sheet of paper with the shortest line coming from the center of the square alternately closer then further away from you. At these times, the figure appears three-dimensional. Also, from time to time different figures will appear to attract your attention. Sometimes the four large triangles will seem dominant, while at other times you will focus on the smaller triangles. As you continue to stare at the figure, various combinations of triangles will, from moment to moment, attract your attention, but you will find that you are not able to focus on a given pattern for more than a second or so.

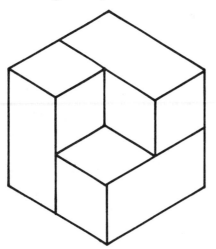

Figure 3.11 seems to be an object which is made up of at least three bricks. At the center one sees a cube. The problem is that the cube sometimes appears to be recessed from the surfaces of the bricks, and at other times seems to be solid with the bricks serving as a backdrop.

Figure 3.11 — Is there a solid cube at the center?

Examples of unstable figures can be found in many tile designs. Thus, one can find each of the two "target" shapes in the title designs in Figures 3.12 and 3.13, and by staring at the figures for a few seconds the target will go in and out of conscious perception.

Figure 3.12 – Can you focus on the target figure in this design above?

Figure 3.13 – Can you focus on the target figure in this design above?

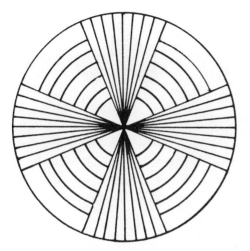

Figure 3.14 – Are the circular lines in front of or behind the radial lines?

That the effect of instability depends heavily on having equally good figures is shown in Figure 3.14. Here, most people see concentric circles behind radiating lines. With some effort, you can see the "pie-shaped" arcs as being over a continuous series of "spokes." However, because the arcs seem to continue behind the radial spokes, this figure tends to dominate.

Figure 3.15 – Are the circular lines in front of or behind the radial lines?

When the amount of space taken up by the black lines becomes approximately equal to the white spaces, there is a strong sense of "visual vibration." (See chapter 19). In Figure 3.15 these very strong spokes and arcs seem more unstable, and it is difficult to focus steadily on one or the other.

Conversely, in 3.16 the black and white portions of the illustration are equally good forms. They appear to be arrowheads. Because the figures are equally good, sometimes the illustration appears to be white arrows on a black background, and sometimes black arrows on a white background. The perceptual concept of figure and background is the topic of the next chapter. Unlike 3.15, most of the illustrations in Chapter 4 will not be unstable, but they may be difficult to perceive at first.

Figure 3.16 – Are these black or white arrows?

CHAPTER 4

FIGURE-GROUND ILLUSIONS AND CAMOUFLAGE

In most illustrations, we tend to perceive a figure that stands out from the background. In printed material, the figure is usually darker than its background. Figures also tend to be smaller and more regular than backgrounds. Sometimes these principles do not hold, and we have difficulty distinguishing figures from their backgrounds. However, this difficulty disappears when we organize parts of the visual image into a meaningful pattern. When this is done, only the figure and background can be seen, and whatever was seen before is gone forever! Many of the illustrations in this chapter are of this nature. Thus, while the previous two chapters contained perpetual illusions, this one is composed largely of "one-time" phenomena. That is, once you understand what is being presented, your perception changes, and will be fixed on the "correct" illustration.

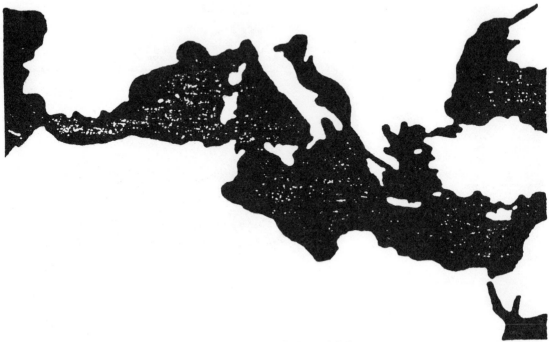

Figure 4.1 – What is this?

Although it may not be immediately apparent, Figure 4.1 is a map. When we look at most maps, we consider the water area to be the background for land masses. On most printed material we assume the paper color to be the background for the figure. Many nautical maps confuse those who are not used to them because the water is the feature of interest, and the land masses define the water's boundaries. In this map, the black area represents water—the Mediterranian Sea. Some people can figure this out relatively quickly because they recognize the "boot" shape of Italy.

Figure 4.2 — What is this?

This is much the same as Figure 4.1. Figure 4.2 is also a map. The black area is again background for the land masses. In this case the black area is the Gulf of Mexico. The southern part of the U.S. is the white space at the top with the state of Florida at the upper right. Below Florida is western Cuba. Most of the white area on the left is Mexico.

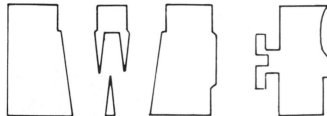

Figure 4.3 — What is this?

In Figure 4.3, one tends to perceive the shapes formed by the lines. Although they are irregular, they form closed figures. When one focuses on the spaces between the figures, the word "WEST" can be seen. Placing a ruler along the top or bottom edge of the figure closes it and makes the word obvious.

Figure 4.4 — What is this?

In Figure 4.4, the black figure takes up much more space than the background. Looking at the black figure, the letter "E" can be seen. It may be easier to see at a distance.

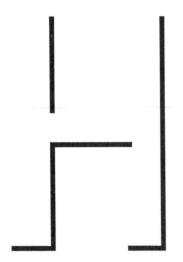

At first glance, some people see only lines forming right angles in Figure 4.5. The black lines represent the shadow of a block letter "H" illuminated from above. Once this is seen, the letter "H" becomes apparent.

Figure 4.5 — What is this?

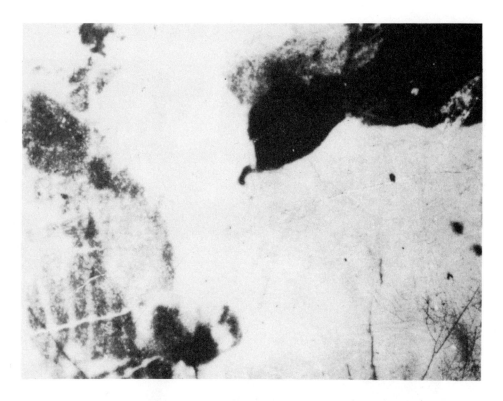

Figure 4.6 — What is this?

In Figures 4.6, 4.7, and 4.8, the white and black areas are intermixed to form both figure and the background. Most people cannot tell what any of them are at first. Figure 4.6 appears meaningless. Once told that it is a picture of the head of a cow, most people can no longer see what they were seeing before! The picture becomes meaningful. Most of the left side of the picture is the cow's head. The dark area near the bottom of the picture, just to the left of the center, is her mouth. You can help people see the cow by showing them where its eyes and ears are. It may help to view the picture from a distance (Dallenbach, 1951).

Figure 4.7 – Who is this?

Similarly, by looking carefully at Figure 4.7, you can see the face of Jesus Christ. Part of his forehead, just above the eyes, is in the top center of the illustration. The right part of his face is in partial shadow, and his hair and beard form the outline of his face. The mottled area on the right is foliage behind him. Most of the white lower center area is a robe, and his right shoulder is in shadow. You may be able to help people see his face if you trace what would be the top of his head in the middle of the picture with your finger.

Figure 4.8 — What is this?

Although the figure is not easy to detect, Figure 4.8 is a dalmation dog. The dog's head is almost exactly in the center of the picture. The dog is walking away from you toward the large dark, curved area in the upper left part of the picture. As a result, its hind quarters look larger than its head. The dog has its nose close to the ground (Gregory, 1970).

While it is not always immediately apparent to people, Figure 4.9 is an ocean liner. The horizontal black area at the bottom is the sea, and the horizontal black area at the top right is smoke from the smoke stack. The triangular vertical black area is the left side of the ship's bow. Your visual position is low in the water with the ship coming toward you (Street, 1931).

Figure 4.9 — What is this?

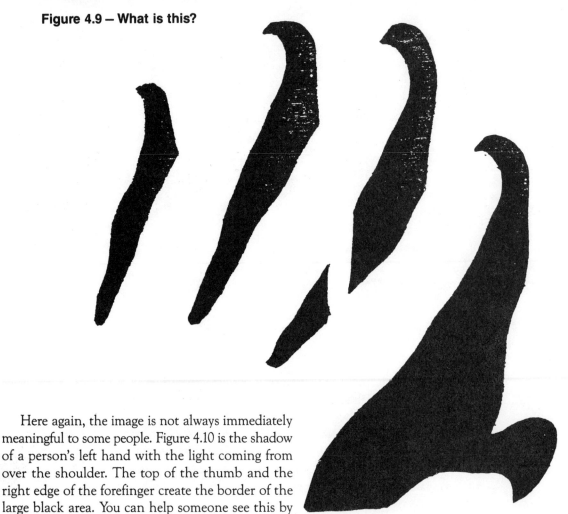

Here again, the image is not always immediately meaningful to some people. Figure 4.10 is the shadow of a person's left hand with the light coming from over the shoulder. The top of the thumb and the right edge of the forefinger create the border of the large black area. You can help someone see this by placing your left thumb in the white area at the lower right and your fingers over the remaining white area.

Figure 4.10 — What is this?

Figure 4.11 — Is there anyone famous here?

The illustration in Figure 4.11 was first presented in the psychological literature in 1951, but it is an illustration that dates back to about 1860. The picture is called *The Tomb and Shade of Washington.* Once again, it is an illustration of figure and ground. Most people do not immediately see George Washington prominently figured in the picture. The reason is that he is formed by the spaces between the tree trunks. Once he becomes apparent, he is difficult to ignore (Charmichael, 1951).

Confusing figure and ground has been popular in art for many years. Figure 4.12 is an 18th century engraving called *The Isle of Dogs.* In some respects this is like the ambiguous figures discussed earlier. The illustration can be seen as two dogs curled up against each other or as two hills.

Figure 4.12 — The Isle of Dogs. An 18th century engraving.

A popular children's puzzle for over a hundred years has been to confuse figures and background in what are called "hidden figure puzzles." Drawings are constructed so that many objects are formed by having common contours or outlines. Figure 4.13 is such a picture. This was the most popular of six such prints by the famous American print makers, Currier and Ives and was published in 1872. It is called *The Puzzled Fox*. Its subtitle is: *Find the Horse, Lamb, Wild Boar, Mens and Womens Faces*. There is something in the picture no longer possible to see in real life. The birds the fox is watching are passenger pigeons—unfortunately a kind of bird which is now extinct.

We think there are at least eight faces in addition to the three animals. It is also possible that there is a cat in the picture, but it is hard to know what the artist had in mind, as opposed to what the viewer is interpreting. Once you find most of the figures, you will be able to see them fairly clearly, but it may take time. Try to find them before you read our descriptions of where they are.

The horse is perhaps the easiest to find. It is in the center of the picture, facing right in profile. The horse's head is turned toward you, between the trees, to the left of the fox's head. The lamb is seated in the lower left-hand corner of the drawing. Its head is in the tree trunk. The wild boar may be the most difficult of the three animals to find. All you can see of it is a large head coming toward you, between the horse's legs.

The men's and women's faces are in the trees and leaves. In the large tree at the left of the picture there are two whose faces are in the tree, and the edge of the trunk makes up the features. A woman's head facing left appears just above the lamb's head, and the features of a man are right behind her. Above this dark face there appear to be two other faces outside of the tree with their features formed by the trunk. One is partly formed by the face of the man in the tree, and the other is directly above it.

The remaining faces are parts of the tree near the fox. One is just above the fox's paw, looking left. The other is just above the first one, to the right, and is looking right. The last two are in the leaves of the tree. The fox's right ear points to one, and he appears to be looking at the other, just above the horse's head.

Finally, although it may be our imagination, there seems to be a cat with striped markings climbing down at the bottom of the second tree in from the left. The cat's head is at the base of the tree, behind the lamb, and his tail can be found further up the tree trunk.

Figure 4.13 — The Puzzled Fox. Find the Horse, Lamb, Wild Boar, Men's and Women's Faces.

Figure 4.14 — An example of natural camouflage.

One of the most important principles of camouflage involves confusing figure and background. Some of these occur in nature. Note how the figure of the snake blends into the cluster of leaves. Attention, the subject of part of chapter 14 also plays a role. Many snakes, such as the copperhead seen here, are also difficult to see because of their complex skin design. Complex patterns of color or black and white on a snake's back tends to attract attention to these areas and draw our eyes away from the snake's head.

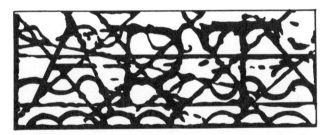

Figure 4.15 — Can you see a word in this design?

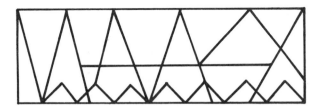

Figure 4.16 — Can you see a word in this design?

Figure 4.17 — Can you see a person's face in this design?

It is important in camouflage to not simply have complex figures. You must be certain to make the background as important as the figure. Note that the word "ART" is easily read in Figure 4.15 even though there are many lines crossing it. On the other hand, the word "WAY" in Figure 4.16 is much more difficult to read since it is closely connected to its background. Similarly, the face in Figure 4.17 is extremely difficult to detect unless you know exactly what to look for.

CHAPTER 5

ILLUSORY FIGURES

In the last chapter, we showed you things that you found difficult to see. In this chapter, you will see some things that are not actually there.

Normally people see lines and shapes as forming a figure, with the paper and white space forming the background. However, sometimes what we think of as background can assume meaning or shape. In each of the illustrations in this chapter, a geometric figure can be seen—even though there are no lines to form the figure! These are called *Illusory Figures*.

Illusory figures depend, in part, on regular "gaps" in the printed figures. When such gaps occur, we tend to try to make them meaningful. One way of doing this is to imagine a regular figure that is not actually there. Often the illusory figure appears to be in front of the printed figure almost as though it were covering part of it. In addition, the illusory figure is usually perceived as brighter than the background. You may heighten this effect in the figure presented by slipping a dark sheet of paper under the page to prevent any interference from material printed on the reverse page.

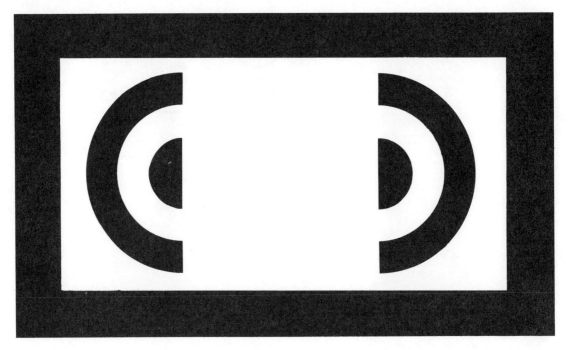

Figure 5.1 – Do you see a square?

Figure 5.1 appears to have a white square in front of what looks like two halves of a target. Although there is no actual printed center square, the curved sections end abruptly at what we perceive as the vertical edges of a square. The effect is heightened by the fact that the distance between the curved sections is the same as their height. This illusory figure is probably the earliest known such illusion. It was introduced in 1904, and is called *Schuman's square*.

While Shuman's square is formed using solid borders, illusory figures may be formed with thick lines, as in Figure 5.2, thin lines as in Figure 5.3, or combinations of forms as shown in 5.4, 5.5 and 5.6. Notice how the illusory figure varies between Figures 5.5 and 5.6 as a function of a very modest displacement of the dots (Parks, 1984).

Figure 5.2 – Do you see a triangle?

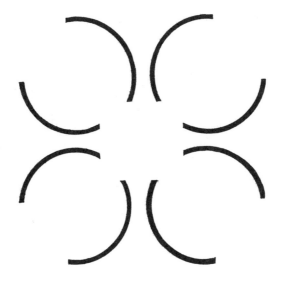

Figure 5.3 – Is there a square?

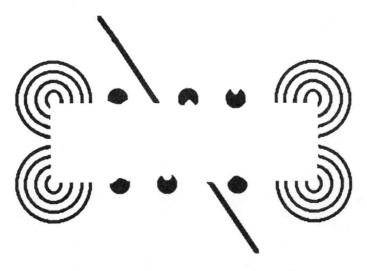

Figure 5.4 – Do you see a rectangle?

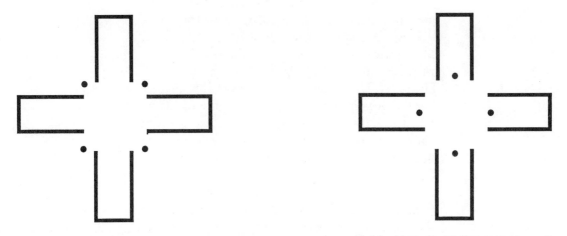

Figure 5.5 – Can you see a cross? A square?   **Figure 5.6 – A circle? A diamond?**

Figure 5.7 — The Sun Figure

Thus far, each of the illusory figures we have presented has been produced by geometric, or at least regular printed images. In 1976, Professor John M. Kennedy of the University of Toronto developed what he called a "Sun figure." It is reproduced in Figure 5.7. Unlike all of the figures in this chapter but the negative image of the Sun figure which he called the "Black Hole figure" in Figure 5.8, the illusory image in the center of the illustration does not have any clear boundaries or contour. Both Figures 5.7 and 5.8 are made up of long strips of dots radiating from a central area. As the strips go out from the center, the dots become more numerous, slightly larger, and form a somewhat more regular pattern. Thus, going from the outside toward the

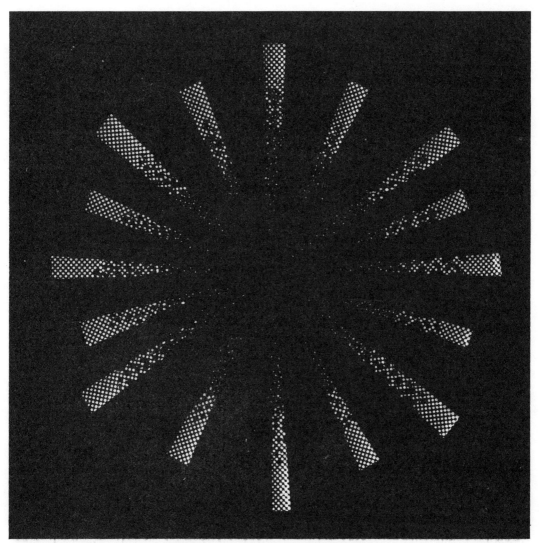

Figure 5.8 — The Black Hole Figure

center, the strips seem to fade. The result is a generally round center, with no distinct outline, which seems to glow.

Professor Kennedy suggested that the effect is stronger if you do not fix your gaze on a single point in the center, but rather allow your eyes to move slightly. He also suggested that the images be viewed under dim light, and that they be seen from arm's length or slightly further. You may need to look at the figures for several seconds to see the effect.

Many people report that the apparent brightness in the center (or increased darkness in the case of the Black Hole figure) seems to pulsate slightly. Some see the center as somewhat misty or like a ball of cotton, and thus it may have a three-dimensional appearance (Kennedy, 1976).

**Figure 5.9 — How many triangles are there?
Eight? Six? Two? None?**

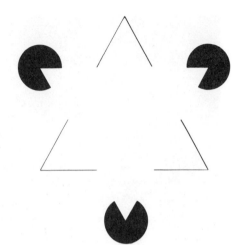

Figure 5.9 has many possible triangles although no triangles have been drawn. The "V" shaped figures can be "closed" by your brain to form one large triangle, or "closed" opposite the apex to form three. The eye can use the portion of the V triangle "underneath" the large white one to close off three smaller white triangles with an apex in each circle. You can also see a six-pointed star by combining the large white triangle and the one formed by the V's. These illusory triangles are called *Kanizsa triangles* after Professor Gaetano Kanizsa of the University of Trieste who first introduced them (Kanizsa, 1976).

Similarly, Figure 5.10 shows that illusory figures can appear with any color surface. Even here, the large black triangle in the center, standing on its apex, appears to be a darker black than the background (Kanizsa, 1976).

Figure 5.10 — How many triangles are there?

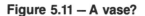

Figure 5.11 — A vase?

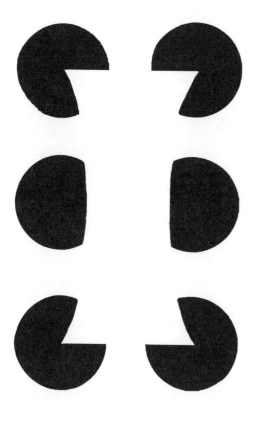

In Figures 5.11 and 5.12 the illusory shapes appear to consist of curved lines. This is the result of the fact that the eye cannot travel in a straight line from the openings in the black pie-shaped figures. By creating slight curves in the wedges, Figure 5.11 appears to be a vase-like figure and Figure 5.12 could be a television screen or a barrel on its side.

Figure 5.12 — A television screen?

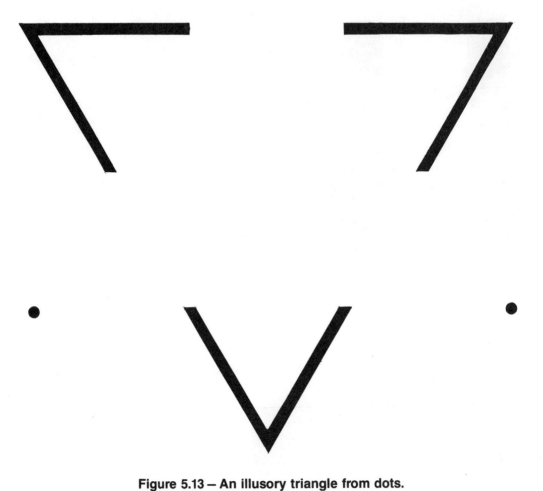

Figure 5.13 – An illusory triangle from dots.

As an illustration of how powerful the effect of illusory figures are, the Kanizsa illusory triangle does not depend upon the pie-shaped figures used in the previous illustrations. As can be seen from Figure 5.13, the use of dots in three corners will still produce the triangle.

Another illusory figure with curved edges is presented in Figure 5.14. In this case, the illusory figure looks like an evergreen tree.

Figure 5.14 — An illusory tree.

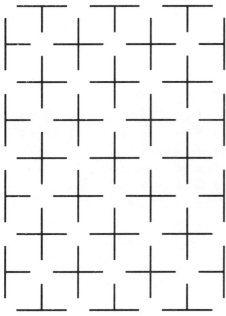

Figure 5.15 appears to be a grid, but none of the lines of the grid touch each other. The empty spaces which would have been their points of intersection are not seen as empty, but as illusory circles or squares which hide the intersections.

Note that if you can see both circles and squares, as you look at the figure the shapes will change back and forth from one to the other. The grid segments are close in size to the illusory figures formed at the intersections. The result is that the eye tends to connect the illusory figures creating a street-like effect.

Figure 5.15 — The "street" illusion.

Figure 5.16 – Illusory circles which disappear at a distance.

Professor Alex Stewart Fraser of the University of Cincinnati created a variation of the grid shown in Figure 5.15. In the top part of the figure one sees the illusory circles associated with the grid. In the bottom half, the lines around a possible illusory circle are almost touching the edge of the circle. The interesting aspect of this illusion is that if you move beyond normal distance for reading the book, the illusory circles in the top lose their brightness, and the circles below seem to be darker than they were. You may see the effect more clearly if you squint at the illustration (Walker, 1988).

Figure 5.17 – Illusory circles with an embedded figure.

Professor Fraser went slightly beyond the previous illustration with the pattern presented in Figure 5.17. You will note that there are illusory circles primarily found at the top and bottom of the pattern. However, there is another figure of circles forming an "X," which you can see if you look at the figure from beyond normal viewing distance (Walker, 1988).

Figure 5.18 — A transparent illusory star.

Illusory figures can also take on an appearance of transparency as shown in Figure 5.18. In this instance, segments of the printed triangles have not been cut away, but have been printed in a shade of gray. The eye perceives an illusory star which appears to be transparent (Kanizsa, 1976).

Still another variation of illusory figures is shown in Figure 5.19. In this case the illusory figure is not two dimensional, but rather a contour. The eye tends to separate the two sets of parallel lines forming a border between them. Either set can be seen as covering part of the other (Kanizsa, 1976).

Figure 5.19 — An illusory contour.

Not only can illusory figures be solid contours, transparent, or two-dimensional figures, they can be three-dimensional as well. Thus, Figure 5.20 can be seen as an illusory pyramid (Richardson, 1979).

Figure 5.20 — Do you see a pyramid?

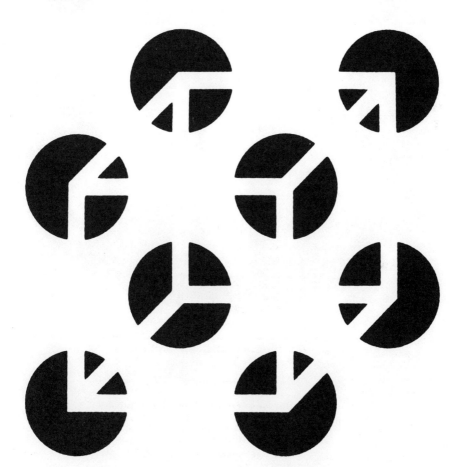

Figure 5.21 — Do you see a cube?

Figure 5.21 also shows a three-dimensional illusory figure. In this case the illusory figure is also the unstable figure called "Necker's Cube," which we saw in Chapter 3. To many people, a cube appears to be in front of the black circles (Bradley & Petry, 1977).

Figure 5.22 – An illusory and an ambiguous figure.

Finally, Figure 5.22 combines illusory figures with ambiguous figures. The white design in the black circle can be roughly characterized as a ship's wheel. It can also be seen as composed of three geometric shapes, a plus sign, an "X," and a circle. As you stare at the figure, sometimes the circle will appear to be on top of the plus sign or the "X." At other times a different figure will emerge as the one closest to you with its illusory outline blocking off the figures below. In addition, whichever illusory figure appears to be on top will appear somewhat brighter than the other two (Bradley & Dumais, 1975).

CHAPTER 6

VISUAL AFTEREFFECTS

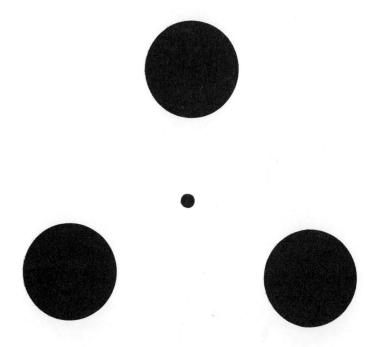

In this chapter you will be asked to fix your gaze on each figure for about 30 seconds. When you look away, you will see something quite different from that upon which you were concentrating. In each case, look at the figure under a bright light unless the text tells you otherwise and then look at a plain wall or a white sheet of paper.

Figure 6.1 — Can you make this light bulb glow?

Figure 6.1 is a black light bulb in a socket. The question is asked: "Can you make the light bulb glow?" You can if you stare at the center of the white filament for about 30 seconds under a bright light. After you have counted to 30, shift your gaze to the blank space to the right of the bulb. You should see the outline of the bulb glowing somewhat more brightly than the white paper itself. This phenomenon is called a *negative afterimage*. It will usually fade fairly quickly, but sometimes you can make it last a bit longer by blinking your eyes. If it doesn't work for you the first time, try staring a little longer.

The negative afterimage is the effect you get when you look at a camera flash. The flash is white, but the afterimage is black. You can also get this effect by staring at any bright light such as a light bulb or through a bright sun-lit window. The stronger the light, or the longer you stare, the longer the effect will tend to last. *To prevent damage to your eyes, be careful not to look at any bright light source for an extended period.*

If you stare at a colored object for 30 seconds or so under a bright light, the afterimage will assume a quite different color. Just as black and white are opposites visually, colors have their opposites as well (called *complimentary colors*) and an afterimage of a colored object will appear as the object's color complement. As we noted in Chapter 1, the *visual spectrum* includes different electro-magnetic waves to which your eyes respond as color. The shorter waves that the eye can sense are in the red family. The longer waves are seen as violet. Waves shorter than those seen as red are called infra-red waves, and those just longer than the longest waves we can visually detect are called ultra-violet waves.

If we take the spectrum, which can be thought of as a straight line of increasing wave lengths, and bend it around so that the longest waves touch the shortest, we can create a *color wheel*. In this circle of colors, the ones opposite each other are the complementary colors. Thus, the compliment of red is blue-green, the compliment of blue is orange, and the compliment of yellow is blue-purple, to provide just a few examples.

Figure 2.21 was the Canadian flag printed in black and white. Had we printed it in its proper color (red), if you stared at it for 30 seconds or longer and then looked away, you would see a blue-green maple leaf, with blue-green rectangles on either side. If you stare at an orange for the necessary time, its afterimage will appear blue, and a lemon will have a greenish afterimage. However, if you try any of these examples, be sure to shift your gaze from the colored object to a white surface. If you don't, the color of the afterimage will mix with the color of the area to which you turn. Even under these conditions, given the laws of the mixture of colored lights, we could predict the color you will see when you develop an afterimage from a particular color, and then shift your gaze to a different colored background.

As you will see in the next several figures, afterimages produce other effects in addition to producing a change in the color of the initial object.

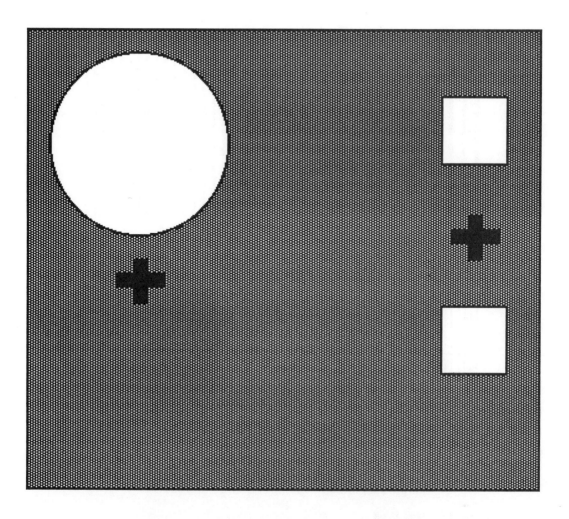

Figure 6.2 – You can make the top square look smaller than the bottom one by staring at the circle.

Not only can aftereffects influence subsequent color perception, they can also influence the perception of size. Figure 6.2 illustrates a *figural aftereffect*. It demonstrates how staring at one figure can distort the perceived size of another. Although the two squares in Figure 6.2 are the same size, if you stare at the plus sign under the circle for about 30 seconds, and then shift your gaze to the plus sign between the squares, the top square should appear smaller than the bottom one. After focusing on one figure for an extended period of time, it becomes the reference point for judging another. Since the circle is larger than the square, the contrast of the circle's afterimage makes the square seem smaller by comparison.

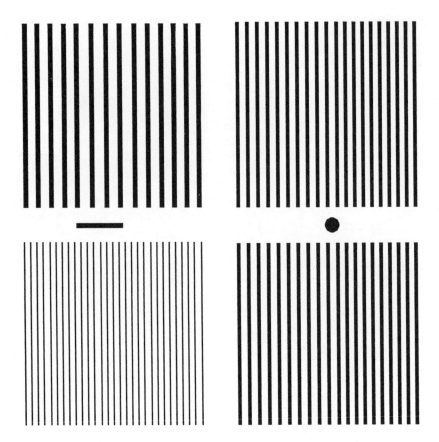

Figure 6.3 — Can you make the spaces between the parallel lines in the left squares unequal?

Similarly, there is a size aftereffect in Figure 6.3. You will note that Figure 6.3 is made up of four square-shaped figures of parallel lines. All of the squares are the same size. However, the square in the upper left-hand corner has darker lines than the others, and its lines are spaced further apart. Conversely, the lower left square is made up of lighter and more closely spaced lines. The two squares on the right side of Figure 6.3 are composed of lines of intermediate darkness and spacing and are identical to one another. If you fixate for about 30 seconds on the horizontal line on the left, and then shift your gaze to the dot on the right, the parallel lines in the top right square will appear to be closer together than those in the square below it. This is known as the Blakemore-Sutton aftereffect (Blakemore & Sutton, 1970).

Afterimages can also change apparent space. In Figure 6.4, the four white squares are spaced equally from one another. If you stare at the "x" next to the middle black rectangle for 30 seconds, and then fix your gaze on the "x" in the center of the white squares, the vertical distance between the left-hand pair of squares will seem greater than the distance between the right-hand pair. The effect may be greater if you cover the white squares when you look at the black rectangle, and cover the rectangles when you shift to the squares.

What you should see in the afterimage is a white rectangle between the two left-hand squares, and one white rectangle above the right-hand squares and one below. The single rectangle between the squares seems to repel them so that they look somewhat further apart, while the pair of rectangles on either side of the squares seems to push them together (Kohler & Wallach, 1944).

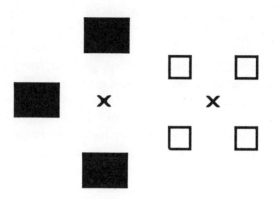

Figure 6.4 — Can you change the distances between the white squares?

**Figure 6.5 — You can change this figure to white
—brighter than the page!**

You may have noticed that as you stare at each of the figures in this chapter there is a slight "vibration" at the edges. This can be seen quite clearly in Figure 6.5. If you focus on the small dot for about 30 seconds, you will gradually notice a "halo" of white building just outside of the dot. While your focus is on this central dot, you may become aware of a similar vibrating halo developing around each of the larger circles. These halos are evidence that the afterimage is developing. An interesting thing about the afterimage is that when you shift your gaze to the white surface to see the pattern in white rather than black, the afterimage will appear to be a brighter white than the background! (Wade, 1982)

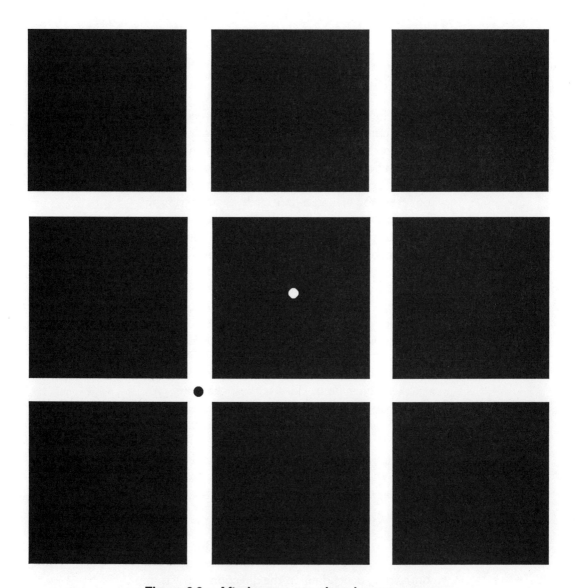

Figure 6.6 — Afterimages can show how your eyes are always moving.

Part of the vibration of the "halos" which you see in many of these figures is evidence that your eyes are constantly making tiny uncontrollable movements.

If you stare at the center white dot in Figure 6.6 for about 30 seconds to develop an afterimage, and then shift your gaze and focus on the small black dot just below it to the left, the afterimage will appear to be jumping around. This is because your eyes are constantly moving, even though you are trying to keep them fixed on the small black dot.

One interesting note about afterimages is that you can change their apparent size depending upon where you look when you are experiencing them. For example, suppose you create an afterimage of the sun by looking at it *very briefly* so as not to damage your eyes. You will see a dark circle as an afterimage. If you focus on your finger held only a few inches from your face, the afterimage will seem quite small. If you focus on a book a foot or so away, it will appear larger. If you look at the wall across a large room, the afterimage will seem very large indeed! Effectively what you are doing is "projecting" the afterimage much in the way a film projector makes an image larger by focusing it on a distant surface.

The last two illusions in this chapter deal with *movement aftereffects*. To see these illusions, you should photocopy Figures 6.7 and 6.8. Cut each copy out and paste it on a piece of cardboard.. Place a small hole in the center of each circle. Next, take a paper clip and bend it so that the end can be placed through the hole and pointed up in a "U" shape, so that the circle can be spun on the middle section of the clip.

If you spin Figure 6.7 and stare at it for 10 to 20 seconds, the spiral will appear to be expanding or contracting, depending on the direction of the spin. However, if you shift your gaze to a stationary object (your hand for example), it will appear to expand if the spiral was shrinking, or shrink if the spiral was expanding.

This aftereffect is due largely to the fact that your eyes are "pulled" in a given direction by the moving figure. In the case of the spiral, the muscles which control your eye movements move the eye back to its original position as it is either drawn toward the center or pulled to the edge. When you stop looking at the spinning spiral, the muscles are not able to

Figure 6.7 — This spiral can make things look larger or smaller.

stop their action immediately, and your eyes continue to move for a short time. You can see this effect in nature. The next time you are near a waterfall, stare at the falling water for 20 or 30 seconds. Next, shift your gaze to some nearby trees, and they will appear to move upward. You may be able to get a similar effect by standing in the shower and watching the drops of water for about 20 seconds and then looking at the soap dish.

Figure 6.8 – Spin me, I pulsate.

Figure 6.8 has two sets of spiral lines. When you spin the circle, the inside and outside spirals will appear to go in opposite directions. If you stare at the spinning circle for about 20 seconds and then look at a stationary object, you can get a pulsating sensation!

C H A P T E R 7

APPARENT MOVEMENT
AND
SUBJECTIVE COLOR

In this chapter, you will again see things that are not physically present. Movement of certain figures can create visual illusions. We have printed several figures associated with this chapter on page 84. Since you must make them move to see their effects, we suggest you make photo copies of these figures. They should be mounted on cardboard and a hole placed in the middle so they can be spun on a paper clip as we suggested in Chapter 6.

Figure 7.1 – Does this figure move?

When you move this book in a slightly circular motion and gaze at Figure 7.1, "spokes" appear in the concentric circles and seem to rotate with the card. If you make a copy of Figure 7.2 and move it in a

Figure 7.2—Does this figure move?

circular motion while holding it near 7.1 with the book stationary, spokes will appear in both! This effect was first reported in 1876.

Figure 7.3 — Watch the gears.

Figure 7.3 is a variation of 7.1. Once again, when the book is moved, spokes appear in the concentric circles which form the middle figure. In this case, however, the gear-like "teeth" in the surrounding circles also appear to move.

Figure 7.4 — Does something seem to be trickling between the sets of lines?

Another illusion of movement in stationary figures is found in Figure 7.4. As you concentrate on the spaces between the sets of lines, there seems to be some movement of "dots" in the vertical white columns, much like a waterfall, although not all of the movement is downward. (MacKay, 1957).

Figure 7.5 — The Traffic Illusion.

Another example of illusory movement in this chapter is called *The Traffic Illusion* and was developed in 1980 by an Israeli artist by the name of Isia Leviant. The figure consists of radiating lines with a circle in the center. Around the circle are two bands. In the Traffic Illusion they can be thought of as roads. If you concentrate on the circle, you may be able to see tiny specks moving around within each of the roads out of the corner of your eye. It may be easier to see if the light is not too bright. Some people can change the direction of the traffic by shifting their eyes slightly to the right or left in the circle. In part, this illusion is the result of afterimages, and you will see similar examples when you get to Chapter 19.

The next three illusions all involve moving the figure. However, the effect we want you to experience is not apparent movement, but rather *subjective color.* Figures 7.6, 7.7, and 7.8 are all printed in black and white. To see the effects of subjective color you must xerox them, and spin them by placing the straightened end of a paper clip through the center of each. When the figure is spun at a certain speed under moderate light, they often take on the appearance of color, even though they are printed in black and white. They are called *subjective colors* because there are no colors actually there. This can be proven with color photographs of the spinning figures. The resulting picture will only appear gray.

Subjective colors are usually quite light, pastel shades. Some people see the colors easily while others do not. You will have to try several speeds to see which works best for you, and for each figure. It sometimes helps to see the colors if the spinning figure is tilted slightly. One interesting feature of these figures is that if you are able to see the subjective colors, you can often see a different set of colors if the same figure is spun in the opposite direction.

One explanation for the illusion is that when alternating black and white images are rapidly received by the brain it creates a mental code which may be like the nervous system's own color code. Figure 7.6 was designed in 1894, but the first discovery of such colors was made by a German psychologist by the name of Fechner in 1838. He used a disc of rings of black and white spaces of different sizes. He expected to see different shades of gray when he spun the disc, but was astonished to see colors! (Fechner, 1838). In tribute to his discovery, such colors are often called "Fechner's colors." The illusion can sometimes be seen as an electric fan begins to spin, or in the flashing black and white images called "snow" on a television set tuned to an empty channel.

It is interesting that although Fechner discovered such subjective colors in 1838, according to two psychologists reviewing the literature over 100 years later in 1939 (Erb & Dallenbach), the phenomenon had been reported as a new "discovery" at least twelve times since.

Figure 7.6 — Spin me and see colors.

Figure 7.7 — Spin me and see colors.

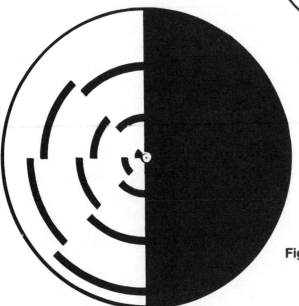

Figure 7.8 — This figure can make colors.

Figures 7.8 and 7.9 also deal with *subjective color*, but they do not require movement for the "colors" to be seen. Figure 7.9 is called the *Luckiesh-Moss* figure, and was first published in 1933. Although it consists only of thin, diagonal lines on a white background, many people see impressions of light colors. These seem to be organized into small hexagonal "cells" which appear at right-angles to the lines. The effect can be somewhat greater under moderate light, and if you tilt the figure slightly. There is no clear explanation for this illusion (Luckeish, 1965).

Figure 7.9 — Can you see colors in this figure?

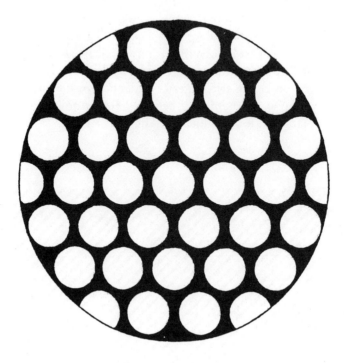

Figure 7.10 — There are colors in the white circles — if you look through a pinhole.

A different *subjective color* illusion was reported by the famous psychologist B. F. Skinner in 1932. It is presented in Figure 7.10. To see the "colors" in this illustration you must view it through a pinhole which you can make in a piece of scrap paper. Look through the pinhole so that Figure 7.10 takes up most of your field of vision. Many people report seeing pastel shades of pinks, greens, yellows or blues. The colors are often reported as seeming to move slightly within the various white circles. While the colors are not strong, they tend to be brightest near the edges of the white circles, against the black background (Skinner, 1932).

CHAPTER 8

IMPOSSIBLE FIGURES

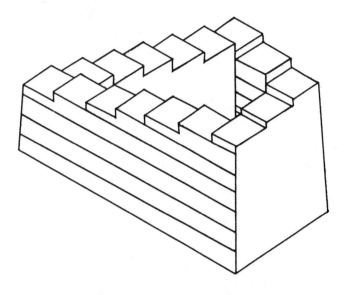

In 1958, two British psychologists, L. S. Penrose, and R. Penrose published an article in which they presented a new form of illusion called *Impossible Figures*. They developed examples of figures that look logical, but which are impossible to manufacture in three dimensions. The Dutch artist, M. C. Escher, used many of the principles of impossible figures in his work.

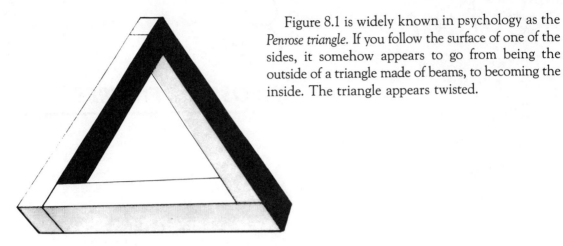

Figure 8.1 is widely known in psychology as the *Penrose triangle*. If you follow the surface of one of the sides, it somehow appears to go from being the outside of a triangle made of beams, to becoming the inside. The triangle appears twisted.

Figure 8.1 — Are the black sides inside or outside?

Other variations of the Penrose triangle using a beam-like structure are presented in this chapter. Figure 8.2 combines three interlocking triangles. Once again, if you trace the surface of any one, you will find you have gone from what appears to be the outside of the beam to the inside.

Figure 8.2 — An impossible figure.

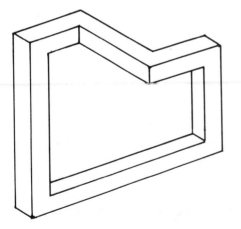

Still other impossible figures constructed of beams are presented in Figures 8.3 to 8.7. In Figure 8.3, the two vertical ends would have to be equal in length for the object to be manufactured, but they are not (Draper, 1978).

Figure 8.3 — An impossible figure.

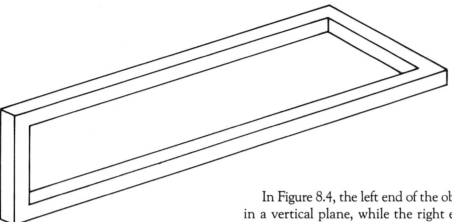

Figure 8.4 — An impossible rectangle.

In Figure 8.4, the left end of the object is oriented in a vertical plane, while the right end is oriented horizontally. At the same time, there is no evidence that the connecting beams are twisted (Draper, 1978).

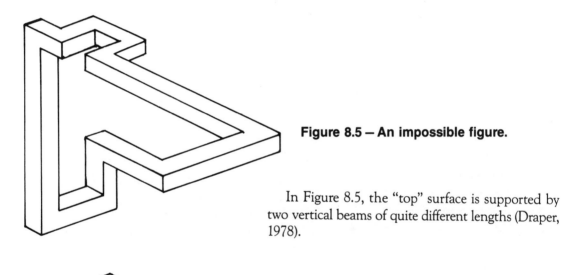

Figure 8.5 — An impossible figure.

In Figure 8.5, the "top" surface is supported by two vertical beams of quite different lengths (Draper, 1978).

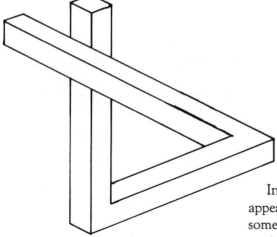

In Figure 8.6, the arm of the triangle, which appears to go from the lower left to the upper right, somehow appears to come back in front of the vertical arm. Such a three-dimensional object cannot exist (Draper, 1978).

Figure 8.6 — An impossible triangle.

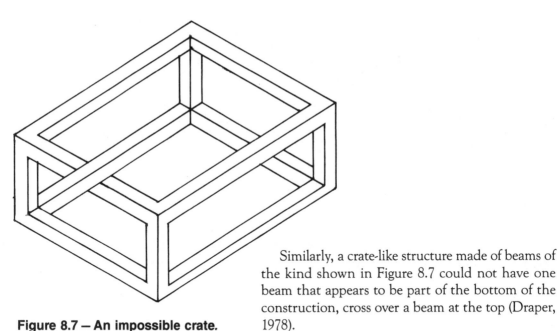

Figure 8.7 — An impossible crate.

Similarly, a crate-like structure made of beams of the kind shown in Figure 8.7 could not have one beam that appears to be part of the bottom of the construction, cross over a beam at the top (Draper, 1978).

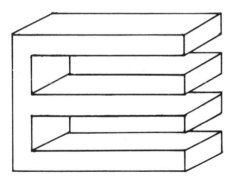

Figure 8.8 — Are there three or four arms?

Similar principles can be found in Figures 8.8 and 8.9. Figure 8.8 looks somewhat like the letter "E" when you focus on the face of the figure. However, when you look at the right-hand edge, there are four horizontal planes (Huffman, 1971). An earlier version of this figure was developed in 1964 by D. H. Schuster, which he called a "three stick clevis." It appears to have three pegs, but has a base which seems able to support only two at a time.

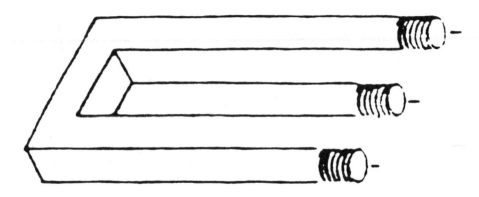

Figure 8.9 — Where does the middle peg come from?

From Roger Hayward, *Mathematical Games* by Martin Gardner, p. 124.
Copyright 1970. *Scientific American*.
Reprinted by permission

Figure 8.10 – An impossible "ancient" ruin.

Schuster's impossible three stick clevis was later
used as the basis for an artist's drawing of impossible
"ancient" ruins shown in Figure 8.10 (Gardner, 1970).

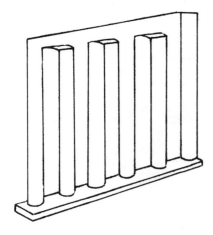

Figure 8.11 – An impossible set of columns.

In Figure 8.11, some of the columns which start at the base of the figure become part of the top beam while some end underneath.

In addition to structures made of beams, Penrose and Penrose developed what appears to be a staircase which would lead a person attempting to go up or down on it to return to the original step after proceeding in a single direction (Figure 8.12). However, if you assume that the base of the figure is a rectangle, you can see that if you extended a line from C parallel to A & B, it would not end under D.

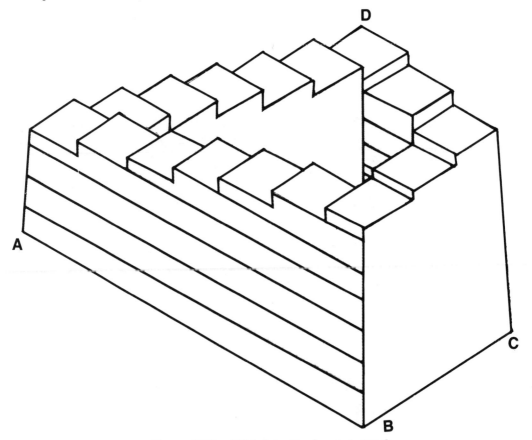

Figure 8.12 – Which is the lowest step?

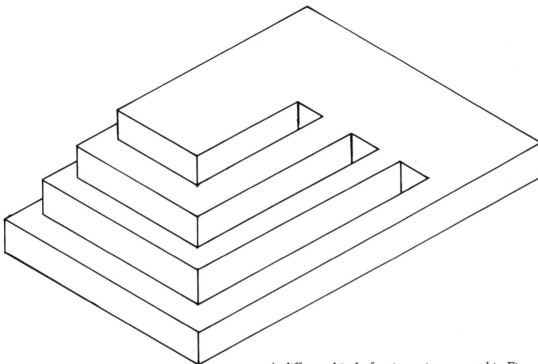

Figure 8.13 – Four steps or one?

A different kind of staircase is presented in Figure 8.13. If you were to walk up the steps starting at the lower left, you would take four steps. If you started upon the upper right, you could make it to the top in only one. Note that the opposite ends of the figure are not of equal length, yet the heights of each of the steps are equal in size.

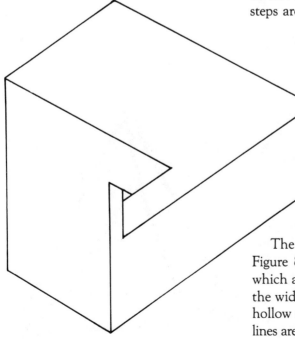

Figure 8.14 – An impossible figure.

The next impossible figures are solid in form. Figure 8.14 is a variation of the Penrose triangle, which appears solid largely as a function of altering the widths of some of the lines so as to remove the hollow area inside the triangle. None of the vertical lines are equal in length, and as a result, such a figure cannot exist in three-dimensional form (Draper, 1978). See the explanation for Figure 8.12.

•

Figure 8.15 appears to be a reasonable figure which would have a pyramid-like shape. It is, nonetheless, an impossible figure. Note that there is a dot above the figure. If you take a straight edge and place it along the vertical lines marked 1 and 2, they will meet at the dot. Placing the same straight edge along line 3 will demonstrate that it falls well under the dot. It would be impossible to construct a solid figure that represents the appearance of Figure 8.15! (Perkins, 1976)?

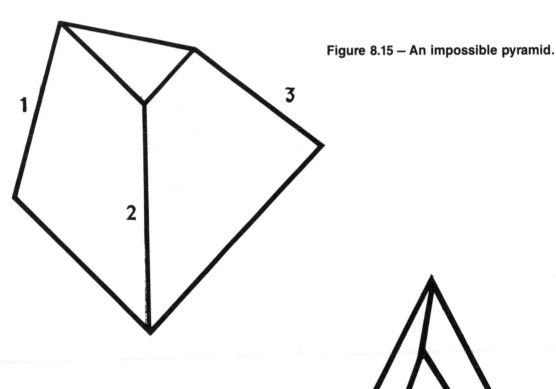

Figure 8.15 — An impossible pyramid.

Similarly, Figure 8.16 appears to be a view of a pyramid-like structure which has been cut off at the top. On inspection, however, you can see that the three vertical lines leading to the inner triangle would not all join at a single point in space (Huffman, 1971).

Figure 8.16 — An impossible pyramid.

The remainder of this chapter presents still other solid figures which cannot be built in three dimensions. Most seem to be reasonable drawings of real objects, but closer examination reveals some anomaly which would make them impossible to construct. Figures 8.17, 8.18, and 8.19 are single impossible figures which have a solid appearance.

Figure 8.17 — An impossible figure.

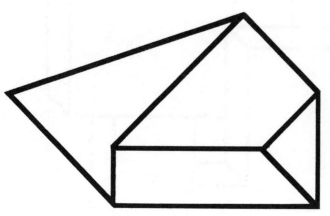

Figure 8.18 — An impossible figure.

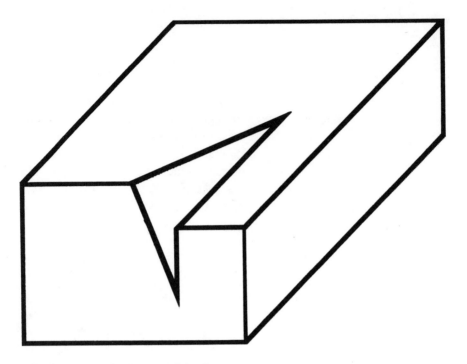

Figure 8.19 – An impossible figure.

Figure 8.20 represents a pair of figures which could exist independently of one another, but not as shown in the illustration (Huffman, 1971).

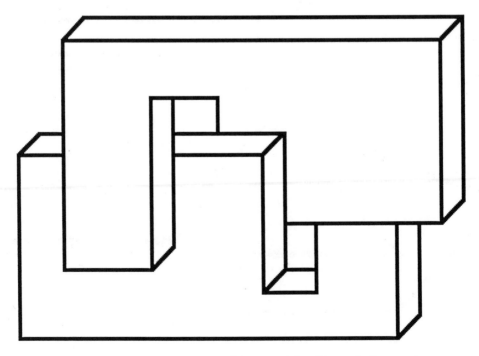

Figure 8.20 – An impossible combination of figures.

Four more impossible figures.

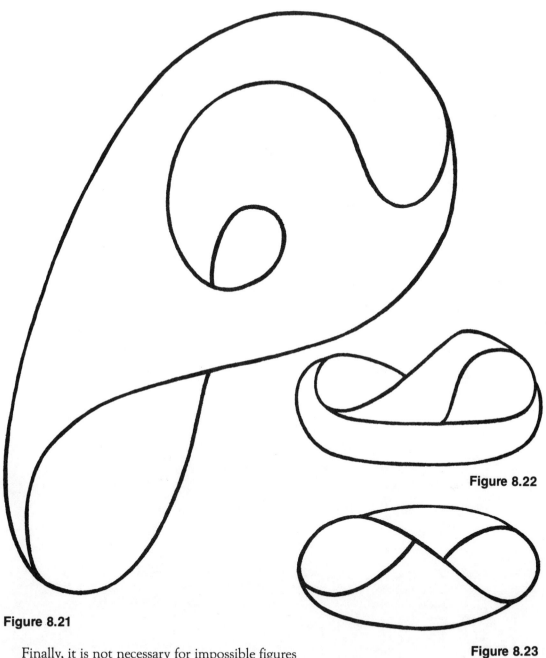

Figure 8.22

Figure 8.21

Figure 8.23

Finally, it is not necessary for impossible figures to be designed from forms which appear to be angular. Figures 8.21 through 8.24 are all smooth objects which cannot be realized in three dimensions (Huffman, 1971).

Figure 8.24

CHAPTER 9

SHAPE DISTORTION

The next several chapters represent fairly traditional illusions. In most, what we see is inconsistent with reality. We have grouped these misperceptions into the categories of shape, size, and length distortion. That is, we make judgments concerning these geometrical properties which are inconsistent with actuality, and although we are aware of our incorrect perceptions, it is difficult to make the necessary mental corrections to perceive the real world with accuracy.

Are the long lines parallel in these figures?

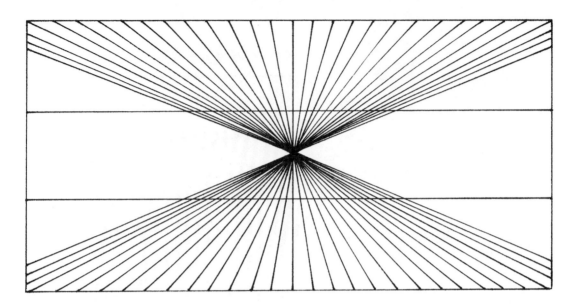

Figure 9.1

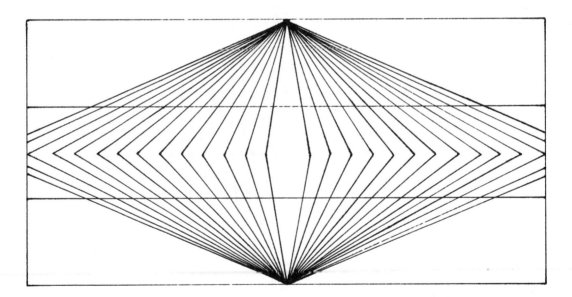

Figure 9.2

Our judgment of shapes can be distorted by the context in which they are seen. Thus, in Figures 9.1 and 9.2, the center horizontal lines are perfectly straight and parallel although they appear to bulge outward in the middle in Figure 9.1 and inward in 9.2. Figure 9.1 is called the *Hering Illusion* (1861).

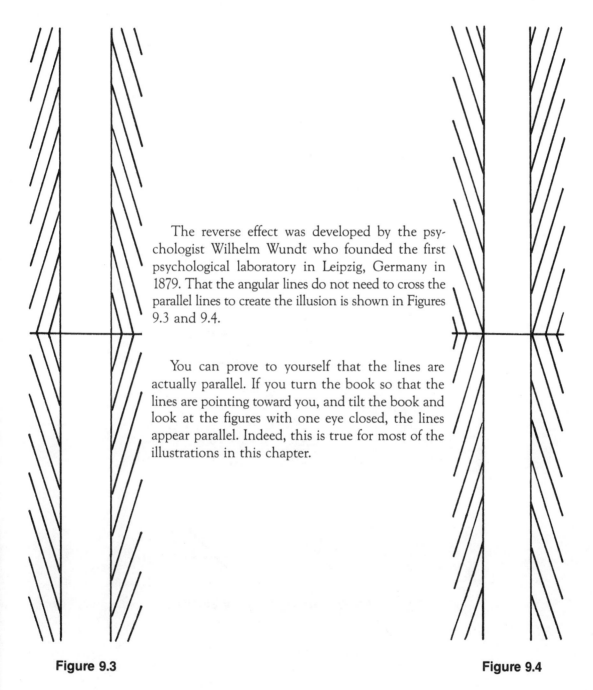

The reverse effect was developed by the psychologist Wilhelm Wundt who founded the first psychological laboratory in Leipzig, Germany in 1879. That the angular lines do not need to cross the parallel lines to create the illusion is shown in Figures 9.3 and 9.4.

You can prove to yourself that the lines are actually parallel. If you turn the book so that the lines are pointing toward you, and tilt the book and look at the figures with one eye closed, the lines appear parallel. Indeed, this is true for most of the illustrations in this chapter.

Figure 9.3

Figure 9.4

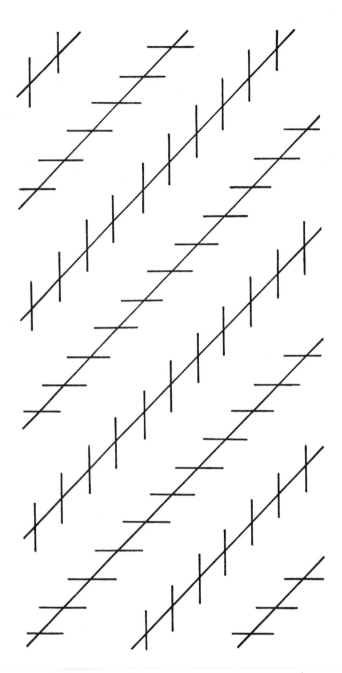

Figure 9.5 — Which long lines are parallel?

In Figure 9.5, although the eight diagonal lines are parallel, the short lines crossing them tend to "pull" them in either a horizontal or a vertical direction so they do not appear parallel. Similarly, Figure 9.6 shows parallel lines which appear to converge as a result of their being superimposed on a "V-shaped" series of lines. One has a similar reaction to cloth woven in a herringbone pattern.

Figure 9.6 — Are the long lines parallel?

An interesting illusion involving shape distortion is known as the *Cafe Wall figure*. In Figure 9.7, the alternating black and white "tiles" which constitute the "wall" seem to have a "wedge-like" appearance, but in fact all of the lines are parallel to one another, and all of the black and white areas are perfectly rectangular. In part, the illusion depends on the thickness and the slight gray tone of the "mortar" between the tiles. The wedge effect may be somewhat greater if you do not look directly at the illustration, but view it out of the corner of your eye.

Figure 9.7 — The Cafe Wall figure.

Figure 9.8 — Are the lines in the circles vertical?

The lines within the two circles in the pattern shown in Figure 9.8 are perfectly perpendicular to the page. Since they are surrounded by lines tilting to the left or right, the eye tends to compensate for this by seeing the vertical lines leaning in the opposite direction (Frisby, 1980).

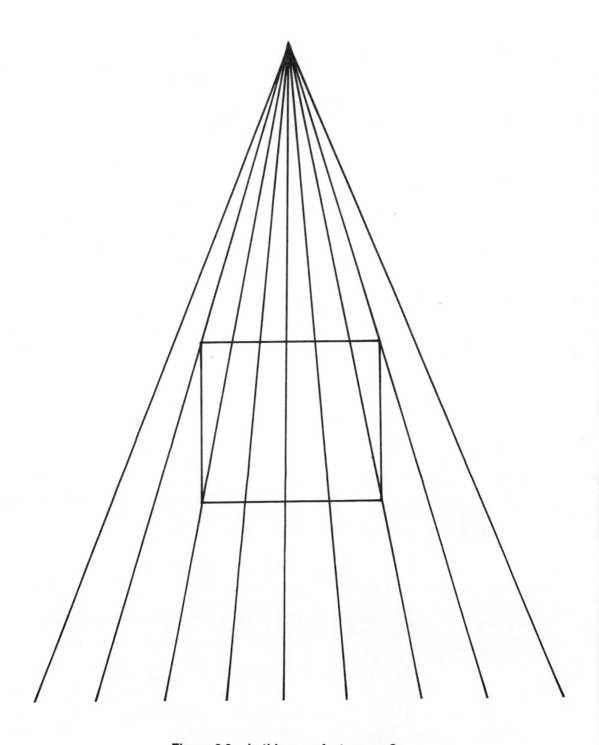

Figure 9.9 – Is this a perfect square?

Figure 9.9 contains a perfect square. The top of the square covers four areas created by the diagonal lines, while the bottom covers six. Thus, the eye tends to see the top as larger.

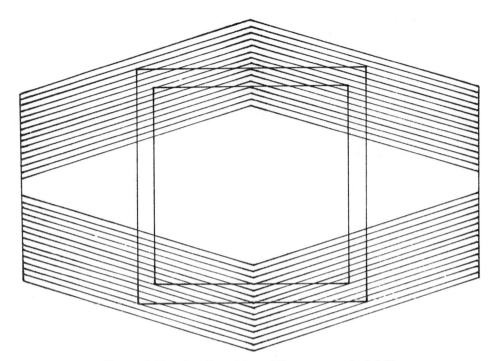

Figure 9.10 — Are the sides of the square straight?

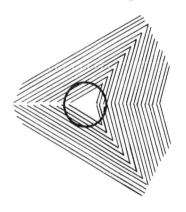

Figure 9.11 — Is this a perfect circle?

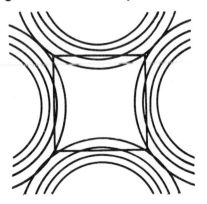

**Figure 9.12 — Are the sides
of the square straight?**

The figures crossed by the "V-shaped" lines in Figure 9.10 are perfect squares. When crossing lines are nearly perpendicular to the figure, as in the sides of the square, there is no shape distortion. When they cross at a sharp angle, they make the straight lines, as in the top and bottom, appear to bend. A similar effect is created in Figure 9.11, where a perfect circle appears distorted by crossing angular lines.

When the crossing lines are curved rather than straight, the resulting figure is distorted in a curved rather than angular fashion. In Figure 9.10 we saw the sides of a perfect square were pushed inward in a "V" shape by crossing lines forming a "V" in the opposite direction. In Figure 9.12, all four sides of a perfect square appear to bulge outward with a gentle curve as they are crossed by arcs pushing in on the square (Ehrenstein, 1925).

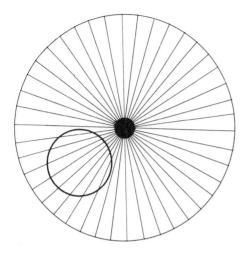

Figure 9.13 — Which circle isn't perfectly round?

In Figure 9.13, both circles are perfectly round. The lines radiating from the center distort your perception so that you cannot easily follow the circle smoothly around the entire circumference.

Shape distortion does not only occur with straight lines as a background. In Figure 9.14, each time the lines of the square cross a circular line, it seems to bend the square. Since the distances between the circles vary as the straight line goes through them, the magnitude of the bending illusion is exaggerated.

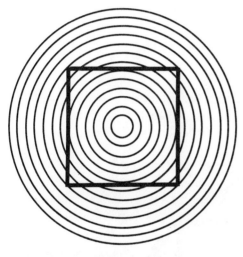

Figure 9.14 — Is this a perfect square?

However, when the square is moved to a different position inside the circles, its apparent shape changes. In Figure 9.15, the vertical sides of the square appear to bend so that their middle areas point toward the center of the circle. At the same time, the horizontal lines are now straight, although they do not appear to be parallel. In Figure 9.14, all of the sides of the square were bowed in different directions, toward the center of the circle. These figures are based on the work of W. D. Orbison in 1939.

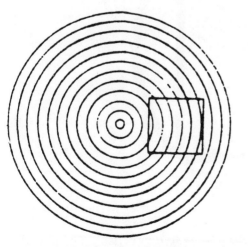

Figure 9.15 — Is this a perfect square?

Figure 9.16 – Does the circle have "dents" where the arrows appear?

Shape distortion can also occur when objects touch each other. The perfect circles in Figures 9.16 and 9.17 appear deformed where they touch the angles.

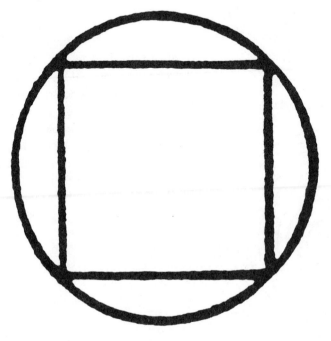

Figure 9.17 – Does the circle go inward to meet the corners of the square?

A   B

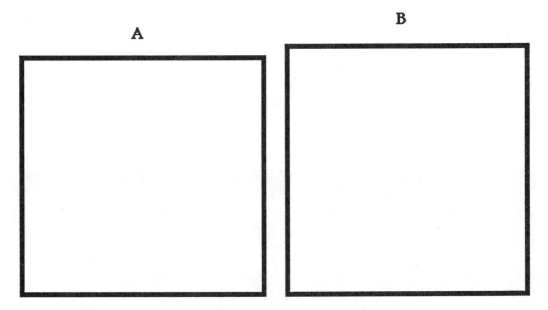

Figure 9.18 — Which figure is a perfect square?

When asked which of the two objects in Figure 9.18 is a perfect square, most people choose "A." Actually, "B" is the perfect square. Because we tend to overestimate the length of vertical lines in comparison wth horizontal ones, we think the vertical sides of "A" are the same length as the horizontal sides. We will show other examples of this in the chapter on length distortion.

Even repeating a simple geometric form can produce a distortion in the true shape of the total figure as compared with the way in which we perceive it. Thus, for example, Figure 9.19 consists simply of a series of arcs, one on top of the other, to form a column. Each arc is of exactly the same size, and thus, the sides of the column should appear to be parallel, but to most people the top of the column appears wider than the bottom (Wundt, 1893).

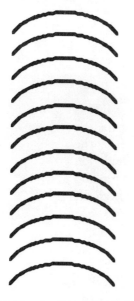

Figure 9.19 — Is the top of this figure wider than the bottom?

Figure 9.20 — Can you make "lift" straight?

Finally, when the color or texture of a line is uneven, the effect may be to distort the shape the line was intended to present. In Figure 9.20 the letters in the word "LIFT" appear to be tilted. You can see that they are not by noting that the top and bottom of each letter are the same distance from the edge of the figure.

Figure 9.21 — Is this a spiral?

Similarly, Figure 9.21 appears to be a spiral. It is actually a series of overlapping arcs. There are several concentric sets as shown in Figure 9.22. Try tracing the largest circle in Figure 9.21 with a pencil point or your finger tip. This illustration is called *Frazer's spiral*. Figures like this were first published in *The British Journal of Psychology* around the turn of the century.

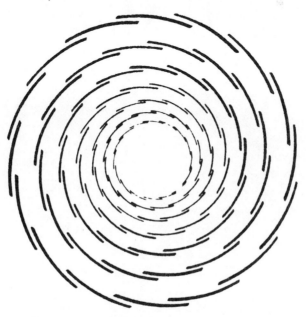

Figure 9.22 — The basis for Frazer's spiral

CHAPTER

SIZE DISTORTION

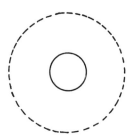 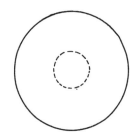

Most people are not good at precise size estimation. Thus, if you ask someone to draw a line exactly one inch long, he or she will probably come close to an inch, but it is not likely to be exact. People are much better at making size comparisons. For example, if two lines of different lengths are placed close together, they are often able to tell which is larger, even when the differences are very small. In fact, when the sense of touch is used, two objects that are only thousand's of an inch different in size can be told apart if they can be touched at the same time.

Despite our ability to judge size differences in many cases, our ability is distorted by a wide range of factors. This chapter will explore some of the things that affect our ability to judge comparative sizes.

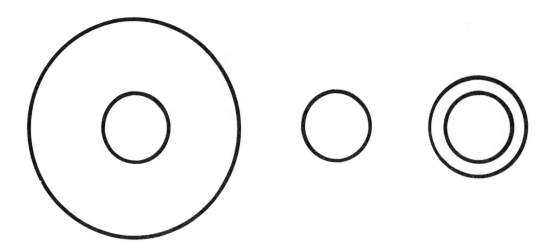

Figure 10.1 – Which inner circle is larger?

In Figure 10.1 all of the small circles are the same size, but one looks larger than the others. The fact that there is an outer circle which is only slightly larger than the inner circle makes the one contained within it seem larger than the circle alone, or the circle with the much larger circle surrounding it. In Figure 10.2, the same distortion is presented using squares. Thus, size judgments may be distorted by surrounding figures. In fact, it has been shown that when the surrounding outer figure is approximately 50% larger than the inner one, the result is maximum overestimation of the small figure. On the other hand, when the outer figure is five to six times the size of the inner one, maximum underestimation occurs. This is known as the *Delboeuf illusion*. It was first discussed in 1892.

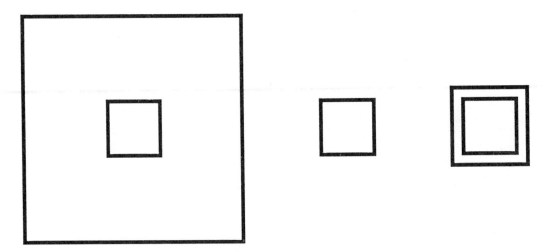

Figure 10.2 – Which inner square is larger?

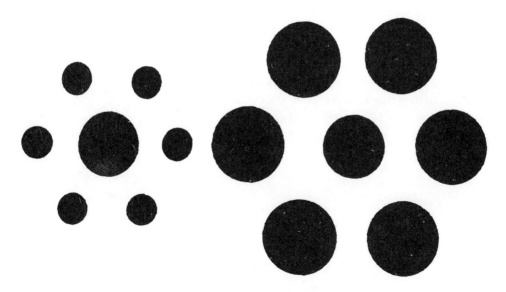

Figure 10.3 – Which inner circle is larger?

However, it is not necessary that a figure be surrounded by another to find size distortion. For example, in Figure 10.3, the inner circles are the same size. However, the one on the left seems larger. This is the result of the contrast in size of the surrounding circles. The same effect is even more dramatic with the squares in Figure 10.4 (Obonai, 1954).

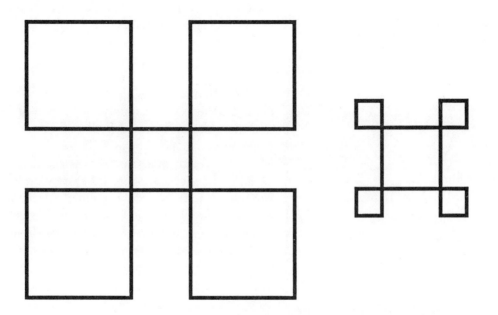

Figure 10.4 – Which inner square is larger?

It is interesting, however, that it is not just the difference in size of the figures nearby which distorts your judgment of the center figure. The center circles in Figure 10.5 are the same size as those in 10.6. In both figures, one circle appears larger than the other. However, the illusion of size distortion is greater in 10.6 than 10.5 when the surrounding figures have the same shape! (Coren & Miller, 1974).

Figure 10.5 – Which of the small circles is larger?

On the other hand, the matter is not only a matter of the comparative size of nearby figures. In Figure 10.5 there are three small circles, each in a different environment. To most people, the small circle in the middle appears to be the largest of the three, while the one on the top seems to be the smallest. All three circles are the same size. While the figure on the top is surrounded by larger circles as was the case in Figure 10.3, the other two small circles are surrounded by arcs. These partial circles would be exactly the same size as the completed circles in the left-hand figure if they were completed. In part, this is the result of the size of the arcs in the middle figure. As you will see later in this chapter, people tend to think that small arcs come from large circles. Also note that there is an illusory circle (see Chapter 5) formed around the small circle at the bottom. (Oyama, 1960).

Figure 10.6 – Which inner circle is longer?

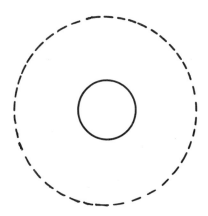
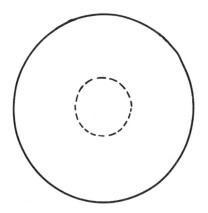

Figure 10.7 — Which inner circle is larger?

To complicate matters further, the two inner circles in Figure 10.7 are the same size, and so are the two outer circles. Nonetheless, the inner circle on the right seems to be larger than the one on the left. In this case, it is not the size of the surrounding figures which distorts our size judgment, but the differences in strength between the inner and outer figures.

Figure 10.8 demonstrates that equal sized circles can be made to appear unequal by the use of larger or smaller squares that either surround or are surrounded by the circles. The right-hand circle seems to be larger to most people. This effect is also apparent with the open-ended shapes in Figure 10.9 where the inner angle seems larger when it is closer to the edge of the somewhat larger angle in which it is enclosed.

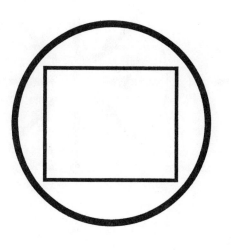
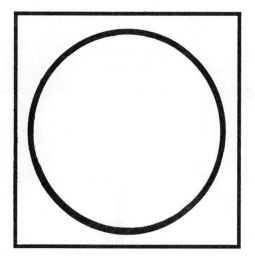

Figure 10.8 — Which circle is larger?

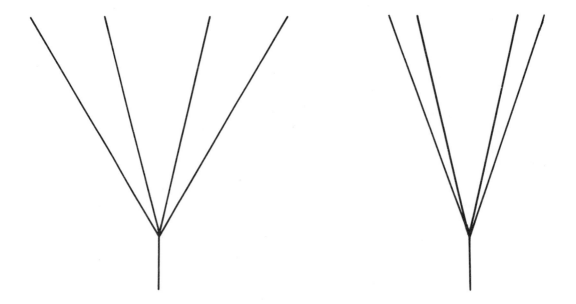

Figure 10.9 — Which inner angle is larger?

A somewhat different effect is obtained in the circles in Figure 10.10. Here, the arrows in the "Inhale" circle segment it and seem to pull it inward so that it appears smaller.

EXHALE   INHALE

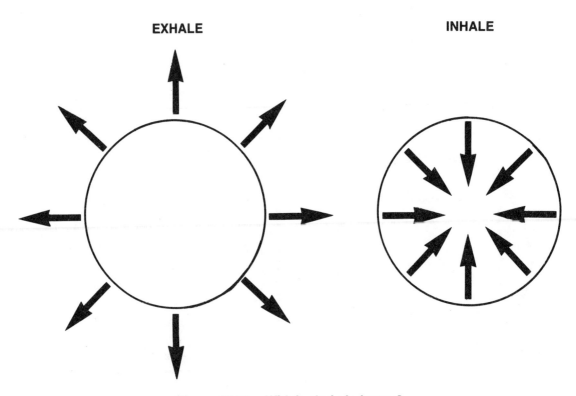

Figure 10.10 — Which circle is larger?

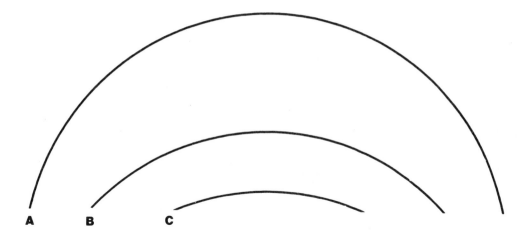

Figure 10.11 — Which arc comes from the largest circle?

Figure 10.11 deals with arcs. The three arcs appear to come from different size circles. However, when you block off the left and right ends so you can see an equal amount of all three arcs, you can tell they are all the same.

Figure 10.12 also uses arcs. It demonstrates that size distortion is not limited to geometrically regular shapes. In this illustration, "A" and "B," once again, are exactly the same size and shape.

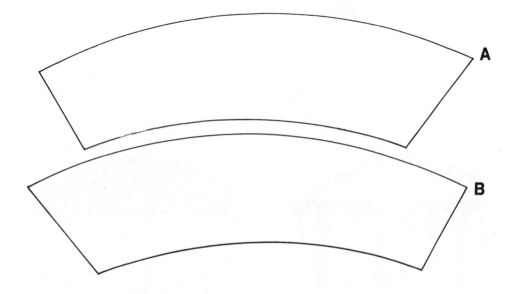

Figure 10.12 — Which figure is larger?

A

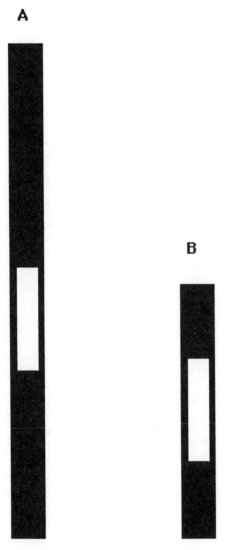

B

In Figure 10.13, although the white rectangles are of equal size, they are perceived as being different sizes because of the contrasting sizes of the black segments.

Further, the columns in front of the two buildings in Figure 10.14 appear to be of different sizes although both are exactly 1/8 inch thick. Columns printed in white against a dark background appear larger than when the building appears in silhouette. White areas and light colored areas generally look larger than dark ones. This illusion is called *irradiation*.

Even the designers of the Parthenon in Greece, over 400 years before the birth of Christ, recognized this. The columns of the Parthenon, which are normally seen against a bright sky, are much thicker than others within the structure, which are seen against a dark wall as a background.

**Figure 10.13 — Which
white bar is longer?**

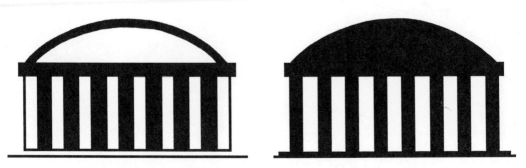

Figure 10.14 — Which auditorium has the thicker columns?

Figure 10.15 – Which square is larger? Which is heavier?

You can see the *irradiation effect* in Figure 10.15. Most people tend to judge the white square as larger than the black one although they are exactly the same size. This is sometimes called *apparent size*. In addition dark colors appear smaller than light ones. If you want something to look slightly larger than it is, the principle of irradiation suggests you use light colors; dark colors will make it look smaller. Sometimes you must correct for irradiation to make different color areas look the same size. The French flag is an example. Because the white rectangle is brighter than either the red or blue, it must be made slightly smaller for the three to appear the same size.

In addition, dark colors appear heavier than light ones. This is called *apparent weight*. If you create a picture with dark colors placed above light ones, it may appear out of balance.

A well-known size illusion in nature is called *The Moon Illusion*. When the moon rises, and is near the horizon as shown in Figure 10.16, it appears much larger than when it is higher in the sky. In fact, the actual image which reaches our eyes is exactly the same. As a result of several different cues with regard to the distance the moon is from us, and the contrasting size of objects on the horizon, the moon appears to be a different size when it rises than when it is high in the sky.

Figure 10.16 – The Moon Illusion

CHAPTER 11

LENGTH DISTORTION

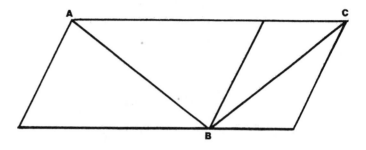

Length estimation also is influenced by context. This chapter presents figures, in which two lengths are exactly the same, but are perceived to be different.

Figure 11.1 — Is the top of the shade longer than the top of the lamp base?

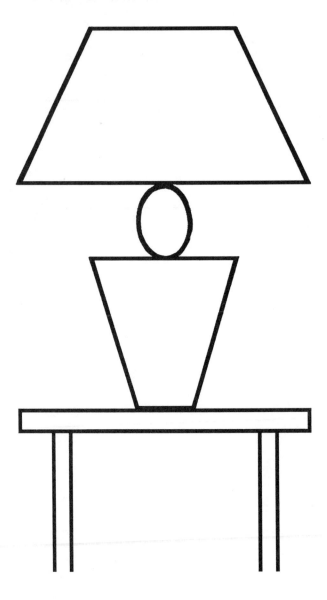

In Figure 11.1, the top of the lamp shade appears longer than the top of the lamp base because of the differing angles of the lines which extend from them. Angles of less than 90 degrees make the enclosed line appear shorter while angles of more than 90 degrees make it appear longer.

In Figure 11.2, the corner of the room seems taller than the corner of the building. Actually, they are the same size. Although we know that most buildings are taller than most rooms, the effect of the angles at each end of the straight line make the room seem taller than the building. The same effect can be produced using lines only. The effect is a classic in the field of visual illusions. It is called the *Muller-Lyer Illusion*, and was first introduced in 1889.

Figure 11.2 — Which corner is taller?   **The building or the room?**

**Figure 11.3 – Which horizontal section is longer?
The Muller-Lyer Illusion.**

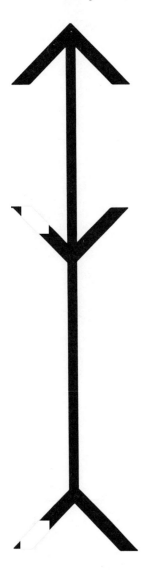

There are a great many versions of the Muller-Lyer Illusion. Probably the best known variation is presented in Figure 11.3. This illusion is one of the most widely studied illusions, in part because the effect is so strong. We will present a number of examples of it in this chapter. Although the two parts of the line are equal, the part between the "wings" is usually judged to be 25% to 30% larger. The amount of error in the judgment depends on such things as the angle of the wings and their length. As can be seen in Figure 11.4, the effect occurs even when there is proof that the distance between arrows is the same.

The strength of the Muller-Lyer illusion is so great you can even place the exact distance between the arrows and the illusion persists. It seems obvious to us that the distance between 1 and 3 inches is shorter than from 3 to 5.

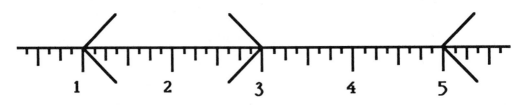

Figure 11.4 – Two inches are not always the same length.

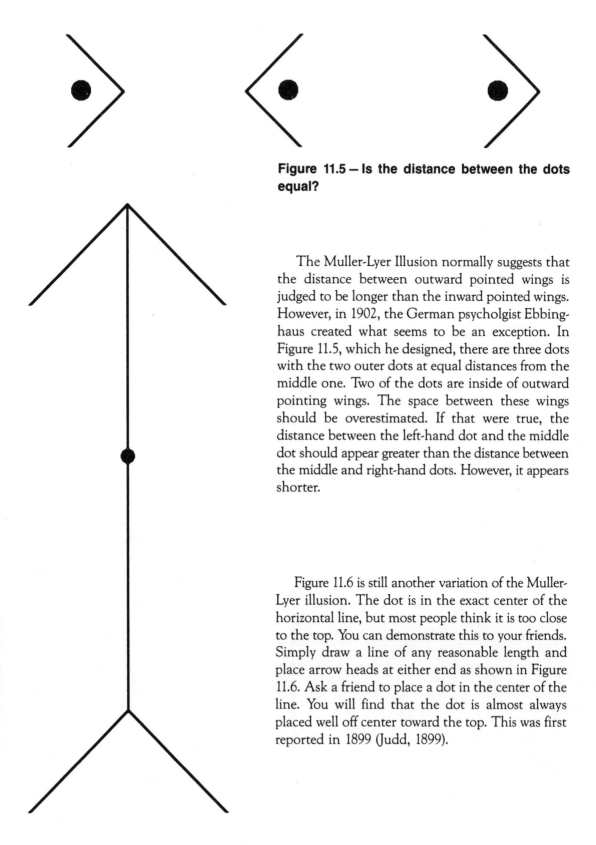

Figure 11.5 — Is the distance between the dots equal?

The Muller-Lyer Illusion normally suggests that the distance between outward pointed wings is judged to be longer than the inward pointed wings. However, in 1902, the German psycholgist Ebbinghaus created what seems to be an exception. In Figure 11.5, which he designed, there are three dots with the two outer dots at equal distances from the middle one. Two of the dots are inside of outward pointing wings. The space between these wings should be overestimated. If that were true, the distance between the left-hand dot and the middle dot should appear greater than the distance between the middle and right-hand dots. However, it appears shorter.

Figure 11.6 is still another variation of the Muller-Lyer illusion. The dot is in the exact center of the horizontal line, but most people think it is too close to the top. You can demonstrate this to your friends. Simply draw a line of any reasonable length and place arrow heads at either end as shown in Figure 11.6. Ask a friend to place a dot in the center of the line. You will find that the dot is almost always placed well off center toward the top. This was first reported in 1899 (Judd, 1899).

Figure 11.6 — Is the dot in the center of the line?

The vertical line in Figure 11.7 seems longer than the horizontal line partly because the eyes move more easily from side to side than up and down. The additional "effort" required to scan a vertical line is interpreted by the brain to reflect greater distance. In general, people tend to overestimate the height of vertical objects. This is an important consideration in many aspects of design.

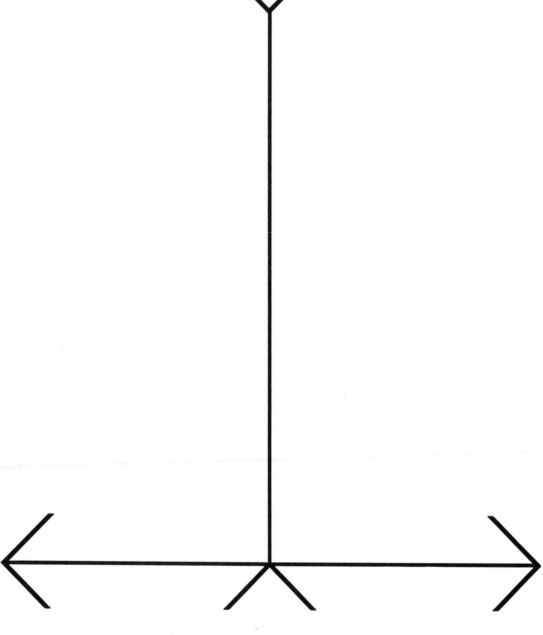

Figure 11.7 — Which line is longer?

Figure 11.8 — The Gateway Arch, St. Louis, Mo. Is it taller than it is wide?

This effect can be seen in the Gateway Arch in St. Louis, Missouri. The height of the arch is equal to its width, but it seems to be much taller than it is wide.

The tendency to judge vertical lengths as greater than horizontal ones does not depend on the use of lines or the arrow-like figures at the ends of lines. Figure 11.9 consists of three dots. The vertical distance between two of the dots seems to be the same as the horizontal distance. However, the distances are not the same. You can see this by turning the book so that the horizontally arranged dots are now vertical. You can also try this yourself. On a piece of paper, simply place two dots alongside each other at a distance of an inch or so apart. Now place a third dot directly above either of these two dots at a distance which seems to be the same as the horizontal distance you chose. It is very likely that you will underestimate the vertical distance.

Figure 11.9 — Is the distance between the dots equal?

EYEGLASSES   **DUMBBELL**

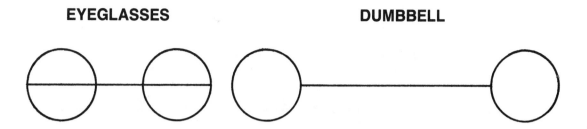

Figure 11.10 – Which line is longer?

In Figure 11.10, the length of the lines is the same for the "glasses" as the "dumbbell." They appear different as a result of two factors. First, the eye is interrupted by the circles in the glasses, and thus the space seems more completely filled. Second, the overall length of the "dumbbell" is greater. As a result one misjudges the length of the lines.

That "filled" space looks smaller than open space is also shown in Figure 11.11 where the distance between "A" and "B" appears to be less than that between "B" and "C." This phenomenon also applies to time perception. Filled time, when you are doing something, usually appears to pass much more quickly than "empty time" when you have nothing to do.

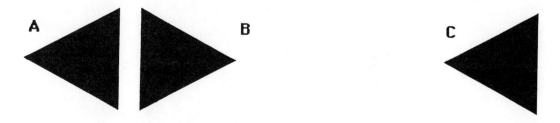

Figure 11.11 – Is the distance from A to B shorter than from B to C?

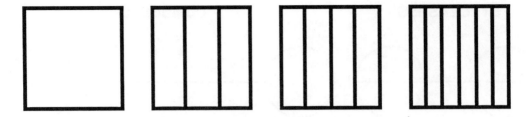

Figure 11.12 — Which figure is the widest?

However, the concept of filling space and making it appear larger is not a simple one. The widths of the several figures in Figure 11.12 seem to become progressively greater. Each figure is a square but as the number of subdivisions is increased, the squares look more rectangular. This was first demonstrated in 1895 and is called the *Opel-Kundt illusion.*

Figure 11.13 — Is the distance between the pairs of dots the same?

On the other hand, although the distance between the two dots in each pair in Figure 11.13 is exactly the same, the distance in the pair with the single line between them appears smaller. A single division makes space appear smaller, whereas multiple divisions make it appear larger!

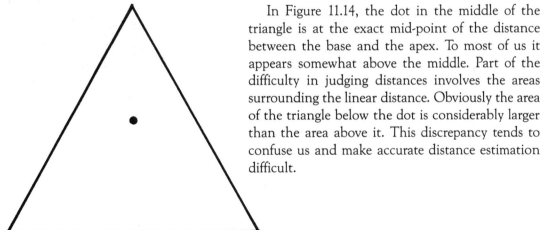

In Figure 11.14, the dot in the middle of the triangle is at the exact mid-point of the distance between the base and the apex. To most of us it appears somewhat above the middle. Part of the difficulty in judging distances involves the areas surrounding the linear distance. Obviously the area of the triangle below the dot is considerably larger than the area above it. This discrepancy tends to confuse us and make accurate distance estimation difficult.

Figure 11.14 – Is the dot half way up the height of the triangle?

That length perception is affected by context is shown in Figures 11.15, 11.16, 11.17 and 11.19. In Figure 11.15, the length of the lines between the two squares is the same. However, when the flanking figures are large they tend to make the line look small.

A similar effect on the perception of the length of the lines of the center segments is shown in Figure 11.16. When the lines extending beyond the center figure are long, they make the center figure appear smaller.

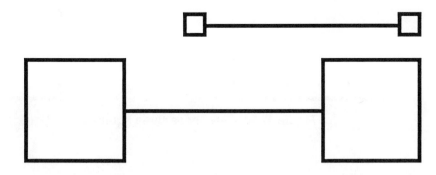

Figure 11.15 – Are the lines the same length?

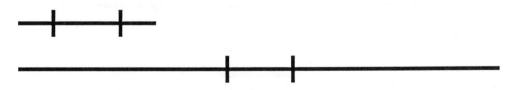

Figure 11.16 – Are the center segments the same length?

Figure 11.17 — Are the spaces between the figures the same size?

In Figure 11.17, the distance between the printed figures is the same for each of the three illustrations. However, when space is surrounded by masses of increasing size it is judged to be smaller.

A similar effect is created with the illusory squares in Figure 11.18. As you saw in the chapter on Illusory Figures, these six lines can be seen as three squares. Although they do not seem to be the same size, they are. The middle square is actually the same size as the other two.

In Figure 11.19, the vertical distance between the parallel lines is the same for each pair. When vertical space is enclosed by greatly differing horizontal distances, the perception of the vertical distance is distorted.

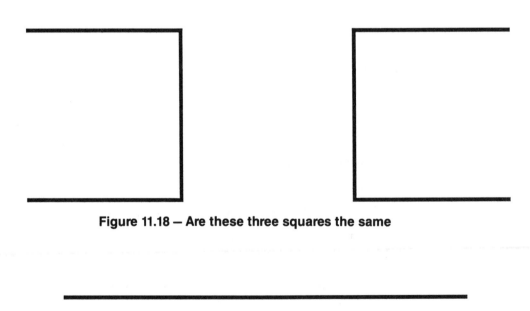

Figure 11.18 — Are these three squares the same

Figure 11.19 — Is the distance between each pair of lines the same?

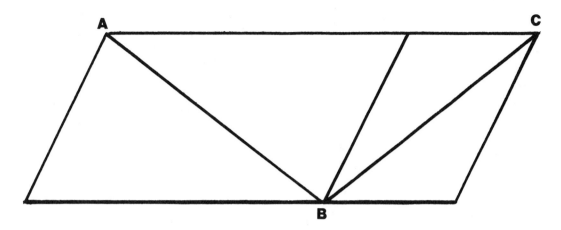

Figure 11.20 — How much longer is A-B than B-C?

In Figure 11.20, line A-B appears to be longer than B-C, but they are exactly the same. This well-known effect is known as *Sandor's parallelogram*, and was first published in 1926.

Figure 11.21 demonstrates that this distortion of length occurs even when the connecting lines themselves are not drawn. The eye still estimates the lengths of the imaginary lines differently.

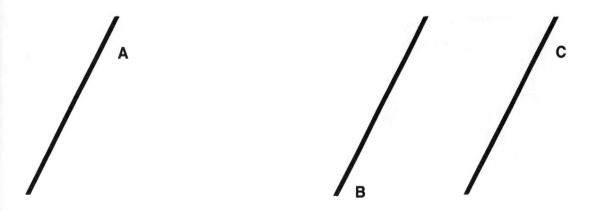

Figure 11.21 — Is the distance from A to B the same as from B to C?

12

CONSTANCY

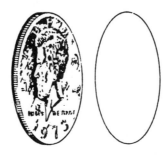

A good deal of visual information enters our eyes that should confuse us, but really doesn't! This chapter focuses on visual phenomena that provide us with misleading visual information, which our brain has learned to ignore or to correct. As children mature, they learn that objects retain their size and shape even when they are seen from different perspectives. However, this can distort our judgments of illustrations.

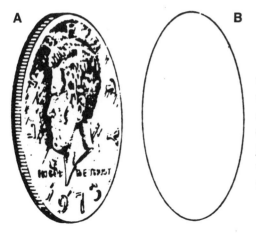

In Figure 12.1, object "A" looks like a coin. Since we know most coins are round rather than elliptical, we judge it to be round although it is exactly the same shape as "B". In a sense, this is a trick question, or a trick coin. Most often we will be correct in judging an image such as "A" as being round, even when the visual stimuli reaching our eyes clearly represents an oval.

Figure 12.1 – Which figure looks round?

Figure 12.2 – Which man is larger?

In Figure 12.2, the smaller person in each picture is perceived to be of a different size. When cues to depth perception such as position in the field suggest that one person is standing to the rear of another, we assume the smaller person is of normal height. This is called *size constancy*. When they are presented on the same plane, the figures are seen to be quite small. Actually, the figures in each picture are exactly the same height. We assume that human beings are of some general size unless we were given information to the contrary. If visual cues also suggest a person may be in the distance, that figure would take up only a small portion of our visual field and thus appear relatively small.

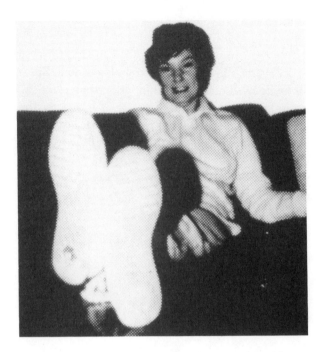

Figure 12.3 — Does this woman have unusually large feet?

Figure 12.3 provides few cues for depth perception. The image is presented in a two-dimensional plane, consequently the woman's feet seem oversized. If more depth cues were present, her feet would appear to be normal in size. If you were in the room with her, you would not perceive her feet as particularly large.

There are no right angles in Figure 12.4! Again, this figure presents a kind of trick question. There are three adjacent diamond shapes which form a cube. Because we know that most cubes have four 90-degree corners on each face, we tend to see right angles even when they are not there. Failure to recognize this tends to show up when persons who are not trained in art attempt to draw familiar objects. In trying to draw a picture of a table top, for example, though some perspective will be included even by someone not trained in art, the top will appear to be more rectangular than the actual visual image. Such a distortion of the visual image in reproducing it is known as *regression to the real.*

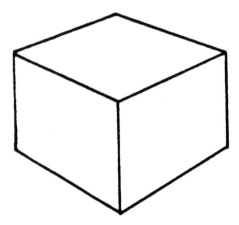

Figure 12.4 — How many right angles are there?

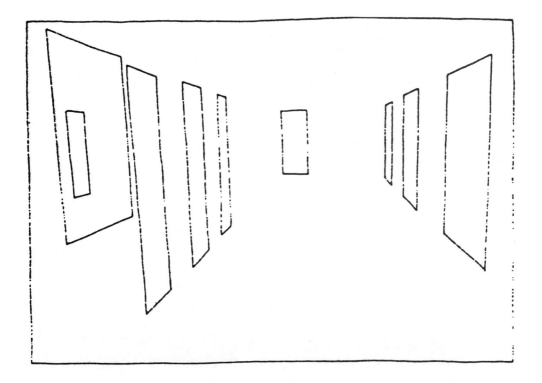

Figure 12.5 — Are any of these figures rectangles?

Looking at Figure 12.5, almost all of the shapes appear to be trapezoids. However, when they are placed in the context of the photograph in Figure 12.6, they appear more rectangular. In fact, if you show Figure 12.6 to people before they see 12.5, they will probably say that they see several rectangles, just as many people see right angles in the previous illustration which looked like a cube. These are examples of *shape constancy*. It is important that we have shape

Figure 12.6 — Rectangular figures distorted by perspective.

constancy to function effectively. For example, can you imagine the difficulty of picking up the right size nuts and bolts if we had to hold each one exactly perpendicular to our eyes before we found the right ones! Shape constancy permits us to take misleading visual information and still make the correct judgments in most real world situations.

Two anamorphic pictures.

Figure 12.7   **Figure 12.8**

There are some examples where shape is distorted, and we are not able to recognize familiar objects. These are especially constructed pictures which are called *anamorphic* pictures. Here common features have been distorted by "pulling" them so that they are stretched in one direction or another. Figures 12.7 and 12.8 are such drawings. To see the drawings properly, turn the book upside down and hold it at eye level, then close one eye and look at them from the top edge of the page. Examples of *anamorphic paintings* can be found as early as the 15th Century. In more modern times painters such as Salvadore Dali used anamorphic figures. Figure 12.7, 12.8—From Fineman (1981).

Figure 12.9 – Traffic markers as anamorphic figures.

Not all anamorphic drawings are necessarily misleading or difficult to understand. In certain situations they can be quite useful. Many municipalities around the world use them to good advantage as road signs (Figure 12.9). If you are seated in a moving vehicle and look well up the road, an anamorphic representation of speed signs painted on the road, or other crossing signs seen from a distance regain their normal proportions!

Figure 12.10 – Is the ring an even gray?

A different kind of constancy is seen in Figure 12.10. The circle is an even gray. However, when a pencil is placed along the black-white dividing line, the part over the white area appears to be darker than the part over the black area. This is called *brightness contrast* since it results from the contrast between the shade of the circle and the shade of the background at any given point.

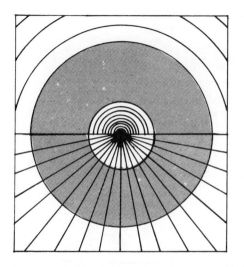

However, you do not need solid and sharply contrasting backgrounds to produce the effect. Figure 12.11 is similar to 12.10, except that there are different sets of lines forming the background for the gray circle. While the circle is an even gray, you can make each half appear to be a different shade by placing a thin line (as thin as a piece of black thread) down the middle. According to two British psychologists, there is greater brightness contrast at the ends of lines than at the sides of lines (Frisby and Clatworthy, 1975).

Figure 12.11 – Is the ring an even gray?

Figure 12.12 – Which gray square looks lighter?

Brightness contrast comes into play again with the two gray squares in Figure 12.12. They appear to differ from one another in overall brightness. However, they are different shades of gray only at the border between them. One side is slightly lighter than the overall shade of gray of the squares, and the other side of the border is slightly darker than the overall shade of gray. If you cover the border with a pencil, the two squares will be seen as the same shade of gray.

CHAPTER 13

DISTANCE ESTIMATION AND DEPTH PERCEPTION

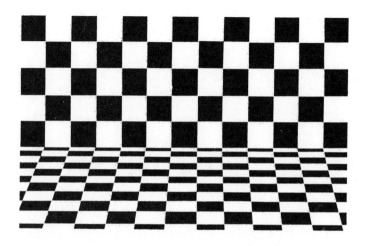

Estimates of distances are usually based on factors related to the concept of constancy, including the visual plane of an object, its size, or its size compared to the size of a familiar object. In these examples we have kept some cues constant and varied others. As a consequence, in Figures 13.1 through 13.4, a different circle is usually judged to be the "closest" although obviously all of the circles are the same distance from you.

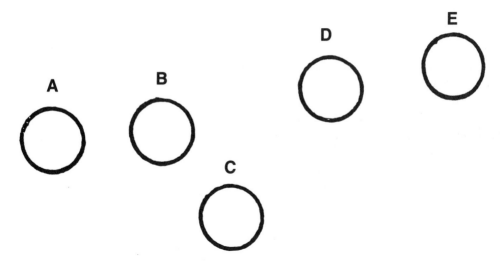

Figure 13.1 – Which circle is closest?

In Figure 13.1, all of the circles are the same size. Most people judge "C" to be closest because it is lowest in the field of vision. Circle "E" is likely to be judged furthest away. In most art, objects that the artist wants to be seen as distant are presented near the top of the picture, with closer objects lower down. Even primitive man represented distance in cave drawings by placing distant objects higher up than close objects.

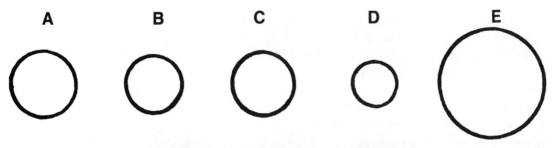

Figure 13.2 – Which circle is closest?

In Figure 13.2, all of the circles are on the same visual plane, but their sizes have been varied. Under these conditions, the largest circle is usually judged to be the closest. "D" would probably be judged to be the most distant since it is smallest. We use the principle of size constancy when we have no other reference point. Objects which appear large are usually close to us, while small objects are often further away. In the absence of other information we use size to make decisions on distance.

If we had five circles all the same size and on the same visual level but different colors, we would make distance judgments as well. Some colors have *apparent distance* as a property. Thus, colors in the red-orange family are usually judged to be closer than most other colors. They are called *advancing colors*. Colors in the blue-green family are usually judged to be further away, and are called receding colors. If an artist wants to create a sense of depth in a picture, he or she would paint objects in the distance in blue or green tones rather than red or orange. The same is true for set design in the theater. For example, if you put bright red objects near the rear of a stage set, it will make the set look much shallower than it is. Pale blue or green objects will make the set look deeper.

It is interesting to note that, in addition to apparent distance, colors also have *apparent temperature*. Advancing colors (the red-orange family) are also called *warm colors*, while receding colors (the blue-green family) are called *cool colors*. Again, the artist makes use of this in trying to convey feelings of warmth or coolness in illustrations.

In Figure 13.3, the cirlces represent familiar objects whose size is known. Although all of the circles are the same size, and on the same visual plane, we know that a golf ball is smaller than the other balls. As a result, we assume that for it to appear the same size as the others it must be close to use while the basketball must be distant. This is another example of using size constancy in distance estimation.

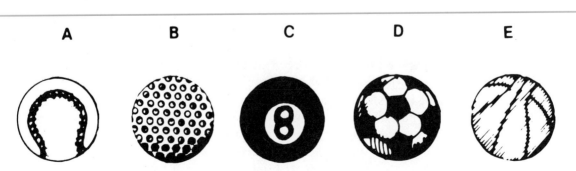

Figure 13.3 — Which circle is closest?

Figure 13.4 — How far away is the circle if it is the moon? Basketball? Wedding ring?

The same principle is illustrated in Figure 13.4. How far away is the circle from the woman? If you think the circle is the moon, you perceive it at a great distance. If you think of it as a wedding ring, it is in front of her. If it is seen as a basketball, it seems to be behind her. You tend to compare figures with the known size of the woman's head, and adjust your perceptual judgment of how far away the object would have to be to keep the proportions correct.

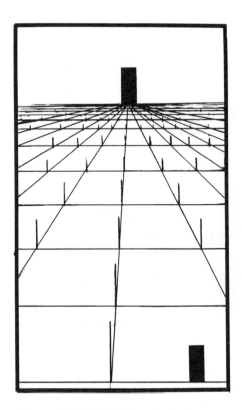

Figure 13.5 — Which rectangle is larger?

There are many cues to the perception of three dimensions from a two-dimensional picture. Not only can we "see" three dimensions on a two-dimensional surface, but such cues may distort some of the perceptions associated with the object we see. Thus, when there are several cues to depth which are consistent with one another, but one which is not, the inconsistent cue is "forced" into consistency by the brain, and seen in a fashion distorted from reality.

In Figure 13.5, the rectangle at the top appears to be larger than the one in the "foreground." They are the same size. The effect is even stronger when you look at the illustration with one eye. Since the converging lines create the appearance of depth in the figure, we assume that if two objects look the same and one appears to be further away, it must be larger.

Similarly, in Figure 13.6, the people appear to be in a corridor. The one who seems to be "furthest away" looks largest, although they are all the same size.

Figure 13.6 — Which person is the tallest?

Figure 13.7 – Which of the two circles is larger?

In Chapter 5, we saw that when there are certain regular gaps in printed figures, we can sometimes "see" figures which are not really there. We called these "illusory figures." We also noted that illusory figures appear to be in front of the printed material from which they are formed. In that sense, the illustration has some degree of depth. Figure 13.7 involves placing a circle on an illusory triangle, and one alongside the triangle. The circle outside the triangle can be thought of as being on the background of the figure. Although both circles are exactly the same size, most people think the circle outside the illusory triangle is larger than the one inside the triangle.

This is much the same effect we saw in Figures 13.6 and 13.7. In each of those illustrations, figures that appeared to be further away seemed larger than identical figures that were judged to be closer. Since illusory figures seem to be in front of the figures that make them up, anything that seems to be on the illusory figure is judged to be closer to you. The circle outside the illlusory triangle, therefore, is thought to be further away. If your eye sees them as exactly the same size (which they are) the brain can only conclude that the one "further away" must be larger (Coren, 1972).

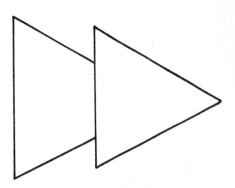

Figure 13.8 is often seen as one triangle covering part of another. It is rarely seen as a triangle and a trapezoid shaped figure. We are more familiar with triangles, and tend to see two of them, in part because the right-hand sides of each figure are the same size. If one triangle appears partly "hidden," then we assume that the complete one is closer to us. When one object prevents our seeing another, it is called *interposition* in depth perception.

Figure 13.8 — Which figure is on top?

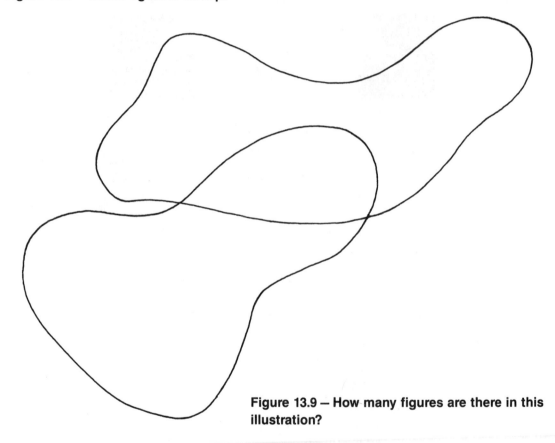

Figure 13.9 — How many figures are there in this illustration?

When asked how many figures are in Figure 13.9, most people will answer "two." It can also be seen as three. A principle of visual organization called *continuity* dominates our perception. That is, certain lines connect more smoothly with each other than with other possible combinations. In this case, *interposition* results in our seeing two figures seen in different planes even though we are not sure which one is on top, rather than three figures all in the same plane.

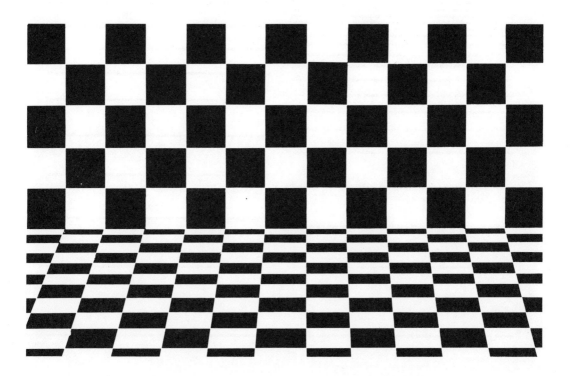

Figure 13.10 — Does part of the figure bend?

In Figures 13.10 and 13.11, changes in the texture suggest depth. In Figure 13.10, the abrupt change in texture near the middle of the figure makes one part appear to be receding in the distance while the even pattern looks flat. Thus, the image appears to "bend" near the middle.

Figure 13.11 — Are these figures curving away from you?

Conversely, the textures in Figure 13.11 change gradually. As a result, instead of bending, the illustration seems to curve away from you. In the right-hand set of lines in Figure 13.11, the curvature takes place much higher up in the illustration. In general, if texture appears coarse, we tend to assume an object is close to us. As it becomes dense, we assume it is further away.

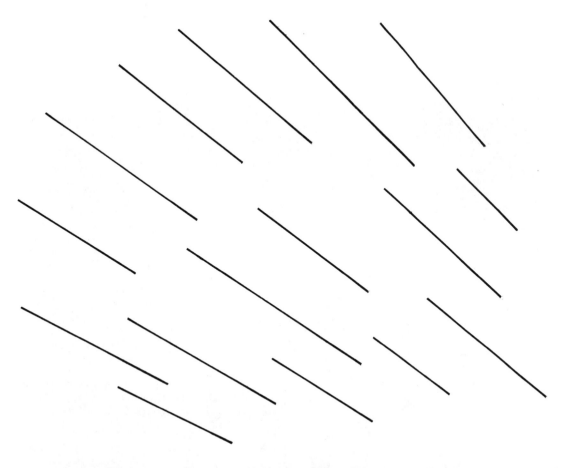

Figure 13.12 — Can you make these lines stick up from the page?

An unusual illusion of the perception of depth is presented in Figure 13.12. All of the lines have been drawn from a point of origin off the page on your lower right. Turn the book slightly clockwise so that this point is in front of you and tip it slightly away from you. Close one eye and look at the figure. The lines should appear to be standing straight out from the paper. This is particularly true if you tilt the book slightly away from you. This illusion was reported as early as 1908 by the famous psychologist William James (James, 1908).

The same principle was applied in the pen and wash drawing on the next page. It was done in 1870 by J. W. Schwenck, and is called "A Castle." (Fig. 13.13) Tip the book slightly away from you and look at it with one eye at the semi circle near the bottom of the page tipping the page slightly away from you.

Figure 13.13 — A Castle.

Finally, when objects are at relatively great distances, dust particles in the atmosphere tend to make them appear less sharp in our visual field than closer objects. This is demonstrated in Figure 13.14. When the atmosphere is unusually clear, as might be the case in a desert, we sometimes believe that objects which are really at a great distance from us are much closer than they actually are. The same lack of dust particles and the cues they provide for distance on earth, make visual judgment of distances in space difficult.

Figure 13.14 — Atmospheric perspective in depth perception.

CHAPTER 14

VISUAL ATTENTION AND ORGANIZATION

We noted in the introduction that early in the process of perception, it is necessary to attract the attention of the viewer. Once attention is achieved, there is a tendency for people to organize the visual stimuli in certain ways. It is these principles of visual attention and organization with which we deal in this chapter. Many of the principles are used in advertising and equipment design.

Figure 14.1 — Is everybody happy?

Figure 14.1 illustrates the principle of change in directing attention. Although there are 77 smiling faces, and only one with a frown, it is easy to pick out the one which is different. This principle is used in designing instrument panels. When an operator must monitor many instruments simultaneously, they should be arranged so that, under normal conditions, all indicators point in the same direction. Under these conditions, if one points in a different direction than the others, it is easily spotted.

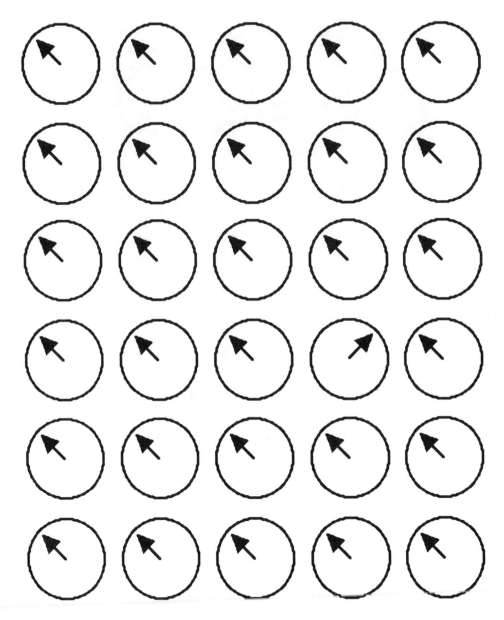

Figure 14.2 — Which airplane instrument is not reading "normal"?

A hypothetical example of this is shown in Figure 14.2. It is easy to detect the one which is "different." An alternate interpretation of this illustration is that the one which is different is actually "normal" and the airplane is crashing! This principle of *change* accounts for the quick detection of a small stain on an otherwise clean piece of clothing.

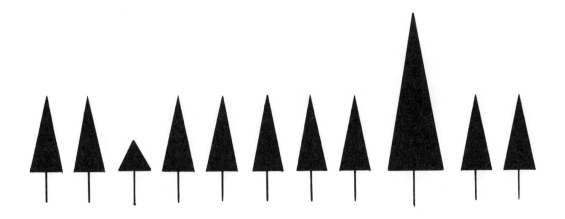

Figure 14.3 – At which tree are you looking?

In Figures 14.3 and 14.4, you can see that *size* and *repetition* are important in attracting visual attention. Comparatively large or small items attract attention. In Figure 14.3, your attention is directed to either the large or small tree. This principle is often used in advertising.

Similarly, repetition, as shown in Figure 14.4, will attract attention. This is true for sound as well as visual images. Thus, a repeated portion of a cracked record pulls that sound into consciousness very quickly. Often, advertising copy will include more frequent repetition of words or phrases than good writing would normally call for in order to increase attention. Similarly, several small ads on different pages of a paper tend to be noticed and read, even if the first one may be bypassed. However, too frequent repetition can become counterproductive as an attention getter. With consistent repetition one tends to adapt to the pattern in cloth; it simply becomes part of the overall appearance. Similarly, the constant ticking of a clock will usually disappear from consciousness.

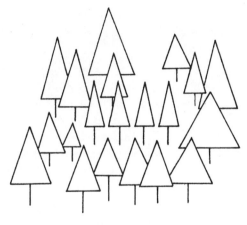

Figure 14.4 – Which trees attract attention?

Figure 14.5 — Describe this illustration.

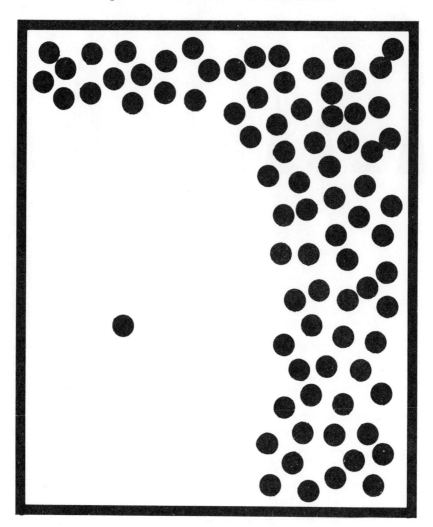

In Figure 14.5 the lone dot attracts our attention. Our visual organization is influenced by the principle of *nearness*. Things which are close to one another are assumed to have more in common with one another than those which are similar but distant.

Thus, the figure might be a performer on a stage, and the audience. One could also imagine that the dots are grapes on a vine, with the lone grape falling from the vine. In almost any description the single dot will be described as having a characteristic different from the other dots, which will all have a characteristic in common.

This perception of shared characteristics also applies to the perception of people who congregate together. This illustration could be titled "The Outcast."

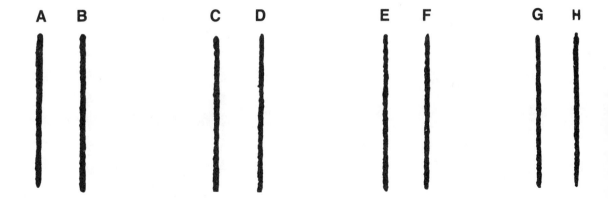

Figure 14.6 — Which lines go together?

Another example of nearness can be found in Figure 14.6. Most people would describe the figure as consisting of four pairs of lines. It is far less common, but just as accurate to describe them as eight lines.

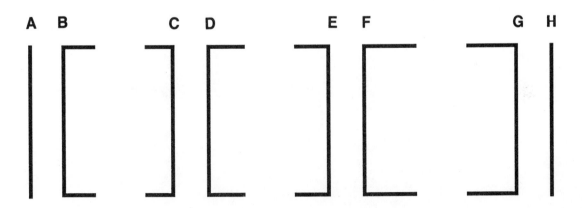

Figure 14.7 — Which lines go together?

In Figure 14.7, however, the vertical lines which were paired in Figure 14.6 no longer seem to belong together as clearly as they did. The horizontal lines begin to form incomplete squares, and the opposite sides of these squares appear to go together. This principle is referred to as *closure.*

Figure 14.8 can be seen as a square composed of smaller squares and circles, or as alternate rows of squares and circles. It cannot easily be seen as columns of alternate rows and circles. This principle of visual organization is called *similarity*. This is also illustrated in Figure 14.9, where one tends to group similar items together. Most people will see the ten circles as forming a triangle, and the three stars as a separate group. Few people spontaneously would describe the illustration as a six-pointed Star of David.

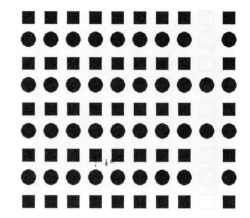

Figure 14.8 – Describe this.

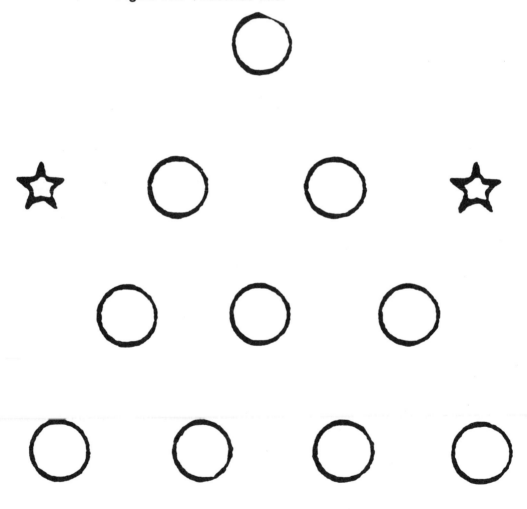

Figure 14.9 – Describe this.

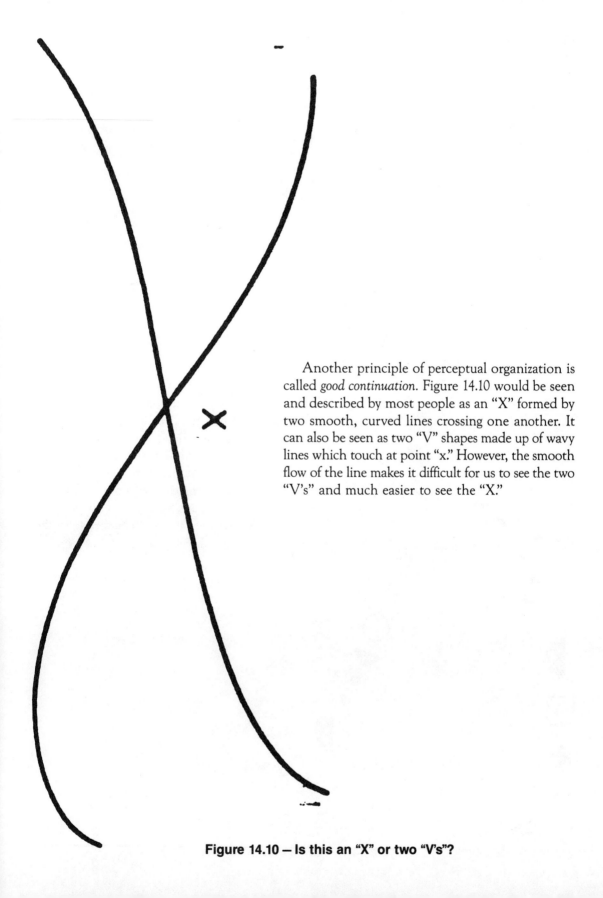

Another principle of perceptual organization is called *good continuation*. Figure 14.10 would be seen and described by most people as an "X" formed by two smooth, curved lines crossing one another. It can also be seen as two "V" shapes made up of wavy lines which touch at point "x." However, the smooth flow of the line makes it difficult for us to see the two "V's" and much easier to see the "X."

Figure 14.10 — Is this an "X" or two "V's"?

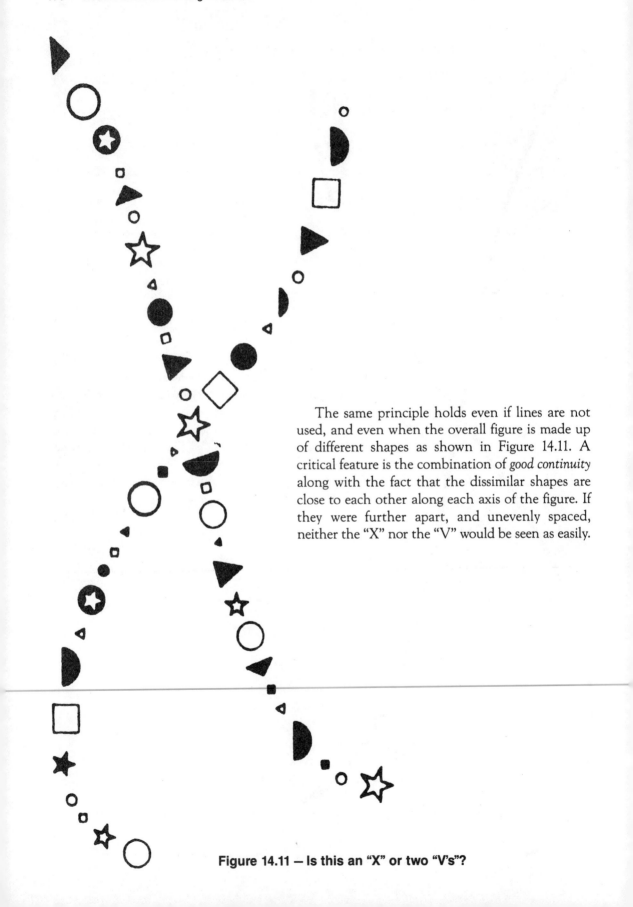

The same principle holds even if lines are not used, and even when the overall figure is made up of different shapes as shown in Figure 14.11. A critical feature is the combination of *good continuity* along with the fact that the dissimilar shapes are close to each other along each axis of the figure. If they were further apart, and unevenly spaced, neither the "X" nor the "V" would be seen as easily.

Figure 14.11 — Is this an "X" or two "V's"?

Figure 14.12 — Do the circles form changing geometric patterns?

Finally, some perceptual organization is based heavily on the principles discussed earlier in terms of equally good visual figures contained in a single illustration. Thus, in Figure 14.12, at any given moment, the white dots within the illustration will spontaneously be organized into different geometric forms such as triangles of three or six dots, diamond shapes consisting of four or more dots, and hexagons with a single dot in the middle.

CHAPTER 15

PERCEPTUAL SET

Perceptions are often influenced by our personal needs and/or our expectations. The well known Rorschach test named after Hermann Rorschach, the famous Swiss psychologist, assumes that if you see certain kinds of images in a meaningless ink blot, they reflect your needs. On a different level of needs, we make use of umpires in sporting events because, even with the best intentions, we tend to see what we want to see. Thus, a close call in a sporting event will be seen one way by supporters of one team or athlete, but quite differently by the opposition supporters. Such predispositions are called *perceptual set*.

We also make use of the context in which something occurs to help us interpret what it is. For example, when we are riding along a straight road on a hot summer day we sometimes think we see pools of water on the road ahead of us when the sun is shining. As we approach the pool, it disappears. Actually what we are seeing are heat waves of air rising from the road. At a distance these distort our line of sight and partially reflect the sky. Since we have so much more experience with water on the road than with heat waves, our first interpretation of what we see in this example is based on what we have seen most often in driving. In this chapter we will present illustrations of how context can influence perceptions.

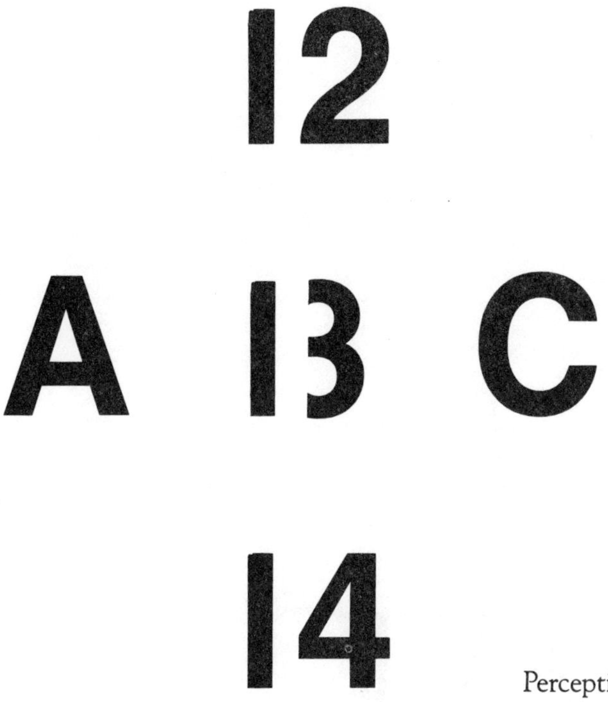

12

A 13 C

14

Perceptions are often influenced by expectations (mental set). In Figure 15.1, the middle figure can be seen as either the number 13, if one looks down the middle column, or as the letter "B," if one looks across the row. Similarly, the words in Figure 15.2 can be perceived as either "bicycle" or as "ride," or both. The shared symbol can be seen as either the letters "cl" or the letter "d." The context in which the middle figure is presented predisposes us toward a certain perception.

Figure 15.1 — What is in the center?

r
i
bicycle
e

Figure 15.2 — How would you read these two words across and down?

Figure 15.3 — What is the center letter?

Mental set is also important when there are slight distortions in letters. Figure 15.3 is a childlike printing of two words. Capital letter versions of the letters "A" and "H" both have horizontal lines. A slight compromise in the straightness of the two other lines which complete each letter, along with context which establishes a set, yields alternate interpretations of the same figure in the middle.

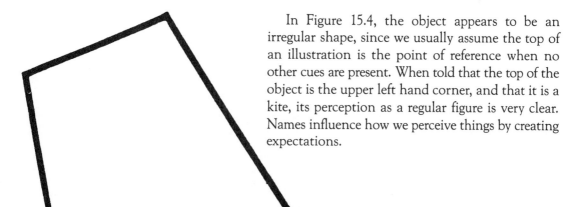

In Figure 15.4, the object appears to be an irregular shape, since we usually assume the top of an illustration is the point of reference when no other cues are present. When told that the top of the object is the upper left hand corner, and that it is a kite, its perception as a regular figure is very clear. Names influence how we perceive things by creating expectations.

Figure 15.4 — Is this an irregular shape?

Figure 15.5 — What is this?

Providing a name made an irregular four-sided figure seem quite regular in the previous illustration. On first presentation, Figure 15.5 has little meaning. In response to the question "What is this?" we assume that the otherwise meaningless forms can be organized in some meaningful way or the question would not have been asked. To the extent that we force some meaning on the lines in the figure, it is likely that the curved lines will have little relationship with the straight lines. However, when the figure is given the title "A Washerwoman Cleaning the Floor," all of the lines in the figure become meaningful. As in many other illustrations in this book, once the figure is given meaning, it is almost impossible to look at it and have the same perception which existed before you knew what it was (Osgood, 1953).

Figure 15.6 — Which way is each man looking?

Even our judgment of where a person is fixing his gaze may be influenced by set. In Figure 15.6 the two men appear to be looking in opposite directions, as suggested by the orientation of the lower portion of the face. But, if you cover the nose and mouth of both men to see only the eyes, you will see that the same drawing is used for each pair of eyes.

Figure 15.7 — What is this?

Figure 15.8 — What is this?

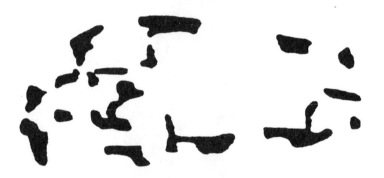

Figure 15.9 — What is this?

Figures 15.7, 15.8, and 15.9 may not be meaningful on first exposure to some people, but when they are told that 15.7 is a musical instrument, and that 15.8 and 15.9 are forms of transportation, a violin, an airplane and a bus are readily seen (Leeper, 1935).

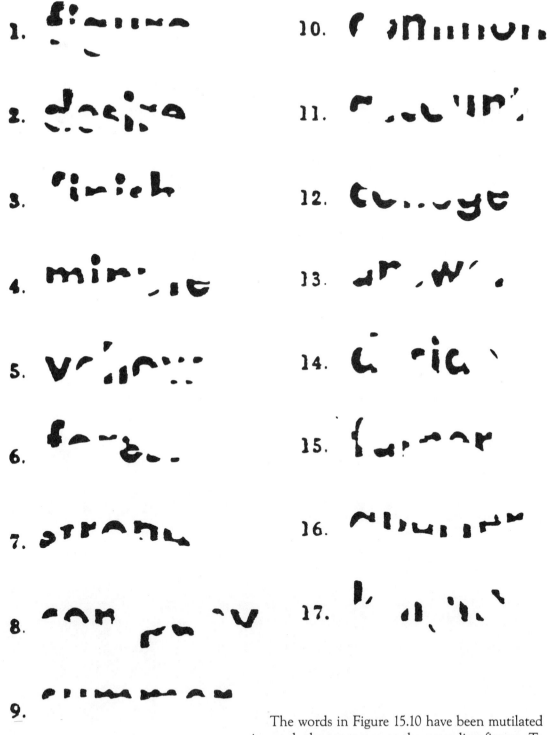

Figure 15.10 — Read these words.

The words in Figure 15.10 have been mutilated in much the same way as the preceding figures. To the extent that one is familiar with words, or, given a hint as to what the words mean, they may be read despite a fair amount of mutilation. Those near the bottom of the list are usually the most difficult to read. The correct answers are presented on page 182.

Answers to Fig. 15.10

1. figure
2. desire
3. finish
4. minute
5. yellow
6. forest
7. strong
8. company
9. summer
10. common

11. account
12. college
13. answer
14. decide
15. father
16. quarter
17. knight

CHAPTER 16

WORD PERCEPTION

When masked at the top it is harder
to read. When masked at the
bottom the result is easy to read

Since the printed word has visual properties, and since the English language is not phonetic, written English is subject to certain forms of distortion. The figures in this chapter illustrate several of the characteristics of words printed in English. Try to read the material in each Figure aloud before you read the text which follows. That way you can attempt to read each one yourself and, after you have done so, you can show each to your friends without clues.

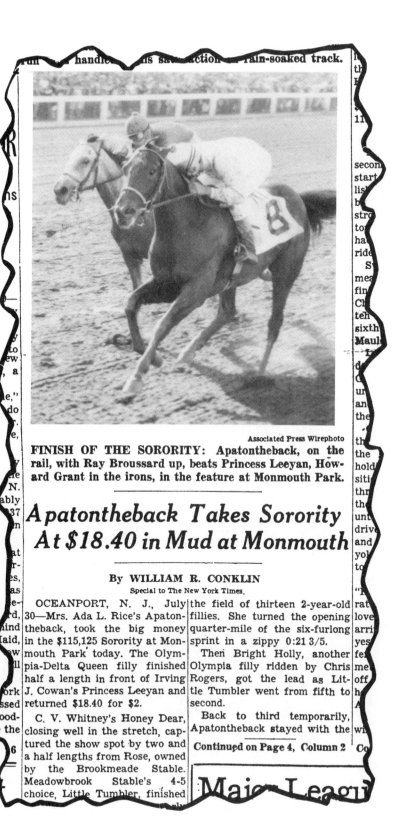

Associated Press Wirephoto

FINISH OF THE SORORITY: Apatontheback, on the rail, with Ray Broussard up, beats Princess Leeyan, Howard Grant in the irons, in the feature at Monmouth Park.

Apatontheback Takes Sorority At $18.40 in Mud at Monmouth

By WILLIAM R. CONKLIN
Special to The New York Times.

OCEANPORT, N. J., July 30—Mrs. Ada L. Rice's Apatontheback, took the big money in the $115,125 Sorority at Monmouth Park today. The Olympia-Delta Queen filly finished half a length in front of Irving J. Cowan's Princess Leeyan and returned $18.40 for $2.

C. V. Whitney's Honey Dear, closing well in the stretch, captured the show spot by two and a half lengths from Rose, owned by the Brookmeade Stable. Meadowbrook Stable's 4-5 choice, Little Tumbler, finished

the field of thirteen 2-year-old fillies. She turned the opening quarter-mile of the six-furlong sprint in a zippy 0:21 3/5.

Then Bright Holly, another Olympia filly ridden by Chris Rogers, got the lead as Little Tumbler went from fifth to second.

Back to third temporarily, Apatontheback stayed with the

Continued on Page 4, Column 2

Figure 16.1 – Read this headline aloud.

The fact that English is not phonetic is apparent when one tries to pronounce the name of the winning horse in Figure 16.1. It is initially difficult for some people. In written language, we leave spaces between words. Because English is not phonetic, the presence of one letter may alter the pronunciation of another. When the horse's name is seen as five words rather than one, it becomes "A pat on the back." This headline appeared in the sports section of *The New York Times* on July 31, 1960. People who are interested in horse racing may not have difficulty in reading the word when they see it for the first time. Writing the names of race horses in this fashion is quite common. A sample of the racing results from three tracks in the New York City area on a single day included the following: Notimeforblues, Honoramongtheives, and Twopairintheair.

"These functional fuses have been developed after years of scientific investigation of electric phenomona, combined with the fruit of long experience on the part of the two investigators who have come forward with them for our meetings today."

Figure 16.2 — How many times does the letter "f" appear in the sentence?

On the other hand, we do tend to associate letters with sound. Most people will underestimate the number of times the letter "f" appears in Figure 16.2, and suggest 8 or fewer appearances. For the most part they will fail to notice one or more of the times it appears in the word "of" because it is pronounced as a "v" in this word. At the same time, they will probably not count an "f" in the word "phenomenon" despite the fact that it begins with an "f" sound. The letter "f" actually appears 11 times in Figure 16.2. Problems with sound influencing reading in English is one reason proofreading is as difficult as it is.

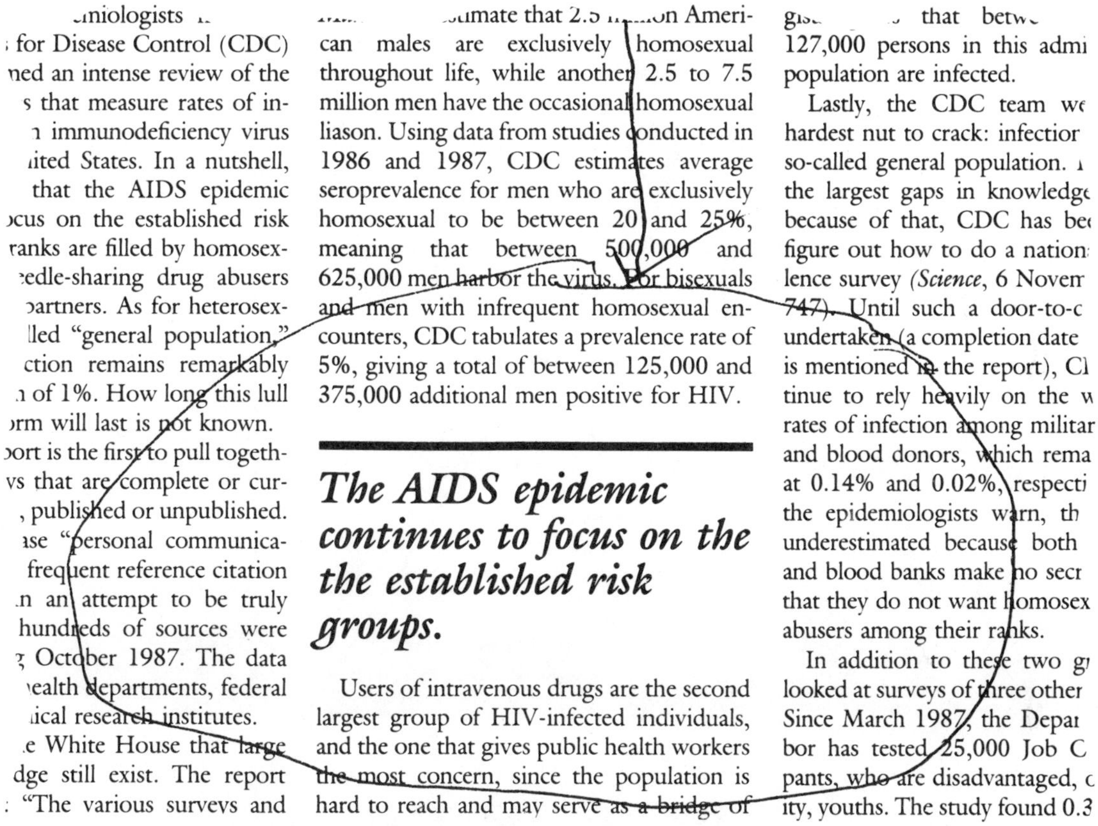

...niologists ... for Disease Control (CDC) ...ned an intense review of the ...s that measure rates of in- ...n immunodeficiency virus ...ited States. In a nutshell, that the AIDS epidemic ...cus on the established risk ranks are filled by homosex- ...edle-sharing drug abusers ...artners. As for heterosex- ...lled "general population," ...ction remains remarkably ...1 of 1%. How long this lull ...rm will last is not known. ...ort is the first to pull togeth- ...vs that are complete or cur- ..., published or unpublished. ...1se "personal communica- ...frequent reference citation ...n an attempt to be truly hundreds of sources were ...5 October 1987. The data ...ealth departments, federal ...ical research institutes. ...e White House that large ...dge still exist. The report ...: "The various surveys and

...umate that 2.5 million Ameri- can males are exclusively homosexual throughout life, while another 2.5 to 7.5 million men have the occasional homosexual liason. Using data from studies conducted in 1986 and 1987, CDC estimates average seroprevalence for men who are exclusively homosexual to be between 20 and 25%, meaning that between 500,000 and 625,000 men harbor the virus. For bisexuals and men with infrequent homosexual en- counters, CDC tabulates a prevalence rate of 5%, giving a total of between 125,000 and 375,000 additional men positive for HIV.

The AIDS epidemic continues to focus on the the established risk groups.

Users of intravenous drugs are the second largest group of HIV-infected individuals, and the one that gives public health workers the most concern, since the population is hard to reach and may serve as a bridge of

gis... ...that betw... 127,000 persons in this admi... population are infected.

Lastly, the CDC team we... hardest nut to crack: infectior... so-called general population. ... the largest gaps in knowledge... because of that, CDC has bee... figure out how to do a nation... lence survey *(Science,* 6 Novem... 747). Until such a door-to-c... undertaken (a completion date... is mentioned in the report), Cl... tinue to rely heavily on the w... rates of infection among militar... and blood donors, which rema... at 0.14% and 0.02%, respecti... the epidemiologists warn, th... underestimated because both... and blood banks make no secr... that they do not want homosex... abusers among their ranks.

In addition to these two g... looked at surveys of three other... Since March 1987, the Depar... bor has tested 25,000 Job C... pants, who are disadvantaged, c... ity, youths. The study found 0.3

Figure 16.3 – Read aloud the large type words in the center of the page from the January 15, 1988 journal Science, dealing with the problem of AIDS.

Reading the sentence from *Science* in Figure 16.3 presents a different problem. Short words, especially those which function as definite or indefinite articles or conjunctions, are not always attended to as inten- sively as are other words. This is especially true when they appear at the end of a line. Even the proof- readers of *Science* did not notice that the sentence contains the word "the" twice in succession.

When masked at the top it is harder
to read. When masked at the
bottom the result is easy to read

Figure 16.4 — What does this say?

Figure 16.4. indicates the relative visual importance of the tops and bottoms of the letters used in
romance languages. In English, and other languages
using the same alphabet, more information is con-
veyed in the "top coast line" of letters than the
"bottom coast line." Thus, Figure 16.5 speaks for itself
by covering either the bottom or the tops of the
letters in the sentences. It says, "When masked at the
bottom the result is easy to read. When masked at
the top it is harder to read."

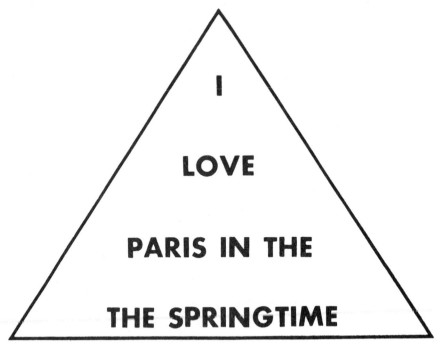

Figure 16.5

This is a real-life example of the more popular
version presented in Figure 16.5. In this case fam-
iliarity adds to the difficulty some people have in
reading the sentence correctly. Since the words "I
Love Paris in the Springtime" are very familiar to
most people, they fail to notice that the word "the"
appears twice.

CHAPTER 17

STANDING ON YOUR HEAD MAKES A DIFFERENCE

Since we most often view the world with our head in a single orientation to objects, we are sometimes unable to visualize how they would appear if they were upside down. The next several illustrations require you to view the figures both as they are printed in the book, and then with the book held upside down, or at different angles.

Figure 17.1 is a reproduction from a deck of playing cards produced in France in about 1800. All of the Kings, Queens, and Jacks are similar to the illustration. In each, the pair of eyes can be seen in 10 different faces: a full face, two profiles in white, and two in black, are relatively easy to find—but then turn the picture upside down and there are five more faces to be found!

Depending on how you hold the book, and whether you focus on the black or white sections, Figure 17.2 has different meanings. Both the black and white parts can be seen as either figure or background. Viewed with the black points facing up, the black area can be background. The white area can be the figure if it is perceived as a theater curtain with the black area the darkened stage in the background. Viewed the other way around, the black area can be seen as a series of tornado clouds against a white lower sky, or, the white area as a figure representing the tops of theater seats with the dark area once again a darkened stage.

Figure 17.1 — How many faces?

Figure 17.2 — What is this?

Figure 17.3 — A hill? A crater?

Figures 17.3 and 17.4 show the influence of shadows on depth perception. We tend to assume that light comes from above. This may be the result of evolving in a world with a single sun above us. There are many animals, most notably fish, with undersides which are much lighter than the top portions of their bodies. Such coloration, sometimes called *countershading*, provides a form of camouflage. Thus, a fish swimming near the surface with a light underbody would not attract nearly as much attention from a fish below it in the water as it would if it had a dark underbody, or even if it was uniformly colored and light came from above making the lower surface of the body appear darker.

Figure 17.4 — Dents or bulges?

it would if it had a dark underbody, or even if it was uniformly colored and light came from above making the lower surface of the body appear darker.

In Figure 17.4, when the shadow is at the bottom, we believe the object is bulging out. When the shadow at the top of the illustration is inverted, it looks like a dent. Similarly, Figure 17.3 appears to be either a hill or a crater, depending on how you hold the book. It is actually a meteorite crater. (From a photograph by D. J. Roddy and K. Zeller, U.S. Geological Survey.)

In Figure 17.5, depending on which side is up, you can see either a young woman or an old clown.

Similarly, Figure 17.6 can be seen as a cheerful policeman viewed one way, or an angry headmaster the other (Frisby, 1980).

**Figure 17.5 — A young woman?
A grouchy old clown?**

**Figure 17.6 — A happy policeman?
A grouchy headmaster?**

Figure 17.7 — Is this a man speaking from a podium, or Abraham Lincoln in profile?

Figure 17.7 is another example of this technique.

In Figure 17.7, the artist has created a figure that looks like a man speaking from a podium when viewed one way, but seems to be a profile of Abraham Lincoln when turned upside down.

Figure 17.8 — George and Martha Washington watching troops, or a portrait of the first president?

Another American president is the subject of Figure 17.8. In this case, the artist has designed the drawing so that when it is viewed as presented in the book, it looks as if George and Martha Washington are watching troops pass their window. Turned upside down, the picture is a portrait of Washington as the first president of the United States. We tend to focus on his face and ignore the inverted figures of George and Martha. (From Kettlekamp, 1974)

Figure 17.9 — Happy or Sad?

Figure 17.9 is a commercial application of the use of such figures. It is a joker from a deck of playing cards advertising Grant's Scotch Whisky. It suggests that whisky can affect your moods.

As printed in the book, the lower 8's and S's in Figure 17.10 seem more symmetrical than the top 8's and S's. When the book is turned upside down, what formerly appeared to be more symmetrical now appears less so.

88888888
SSSSS
88888888
SSSSSS

Figure 17.10 — Which set of 8's and S's looks more symmetrical?

In some respects, our ability to recognize faces under certain conditions, but not others, is a visual oddity. We have a great ability to recognize thousands of different faces. We continue to recognize them even when they are altered as a result of emotional responses such as laughing or frowning. We are even able to recognize familiar faces when they appear in cartoons or caricatures where an artist will distort the features such as size or shape of the nose, the eyes, the mouth, etc.

Figure 17.11 — Who are these people?
Can you name them?

On the other hand, when a familiar face is seen upside down we often have great difficulty in recognizing the person. How many of the famous faces in Figure 17.11 can you recognize without turning the book upside down? The chances are you will recognize very few this way, but all of them when you turn the book over. You can easily make up your own set by cutting pictures out of the newspapers or magazines. Try to stay away from pictures of men who have beards or moustaches. Also watch out for unusual clothing, or unusual hair styles. These cues tend to make it easier to recognize the person.

**Figure 17.11a – Who are these people?
Can you name them?**

Answers on following page.

Answers to Figures 17 and 17a

A) Ronald Reagan B) Richard Nixon C) Elizabeth Taylor D) Elvis Presley E) Jimmy Carter F) George Bush G) Clark Gable H) Gerald Ford I) Humphrey Bogart J) Marlon Brando K) Sylvester Stallone L) Marilyn Monroe M) Leonard Nimoy

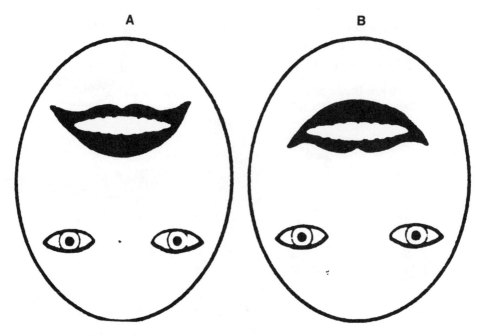

Figure 17.12 — Which face is more attractive? Turn the book upside-down.

As Figure 17.12 is printed in the book, with the mouth above the eyes, most people judge face "A" to be more attractive. When it is inverted so the eyes and mouth have their normal relationship, "A" appears to be grotesque. When we smile, our lips tend to curve upward and upper teeth are revealed. There is a tendency to assume that the top of anything we look at really is the top, unless there are cues to the contrary. When the illustration is inverted, we see the lips curving down, and lower teeth exposed. This is much more an anxiety-provoking facial expression than a smile (Parks & Coss, 1986).

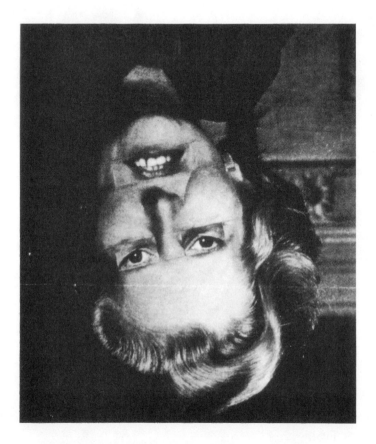

Figure 17.13 — The Margaret Thatcher illusion.

Another example of this is in Figure 17.13. You may recognize it as an inverted picture of Margaret Thatcher. Professor Peter Thompson of the University of York in England discovered that if you take almost any smiling face and cut out the eyes and mouth and invert them in the original picture, when the face is seen right side up it appears quite horrible. He calls this the *Margaret Thatcher Illusion.*

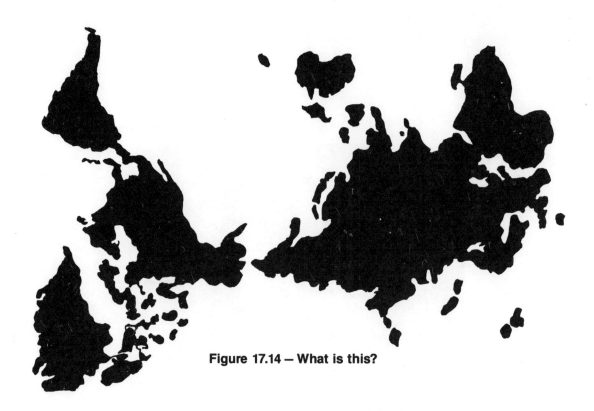

Figure 17.14 – What is this?

Most people will recognize Figure 17.14 as a map, but they will have difficulty identifying the geographic area. When it is turned upside down it is almost immediately seen as a map of the world. It is interesting to note that when Australian college students are asked to draw a map of the world, they draw something resembling the map pictured in Figure 17.14.

Geographer Thomas F. Saarinen of the University of Arizona conducted a study in which he asked thousands of first-year college students from over 50 countries to draw a map of the world. Most drew maps with the North Pole at the top, and Europe in the center. Students from western sections of the United States and Canada tended to put North America in the center. Dr. Saarinen's hypothesis was that students would tend to exaggerate the size of their own continent. However, he found that most drawings focused on Europe, probably because most maps of the world drawn over the centuries have been Eurocentric. On the other hand, Australian students drew maps of the world with their continent on top and in the center, with the North Pole at the bottom (*Psychology Today*, 1987).

An extended version of two different meanings depending on whether the illustration is viewed right side up or upside down is in the work of cartoonist Gustave Verbeek whose works appeared at the turn of the century. Verbeek developed a complete 12 panel cartoon strip entitled *The Upside-downs of Little Lady Lovekins and Old Man Muffaroo,* using only 6 panels. To follow the whole story, it is necessary to turn the page upside-down so that panel 6, when inverted, becomes panel 7. Verbeek did over 60 strips of this kind. We have presented three samples of them here. Although not all of his effects are equally good, and the illustrations have a somewhat dated feeling, they are impressive in that there are two completely different pictures depending on the panel's orientation. Note that he was even able to use letters of the alphabet from both perspectives as in *The Adventure of the Bad Snake and the Good Wizard.* It is interesting that Verbeek was able to tell a complete story using both perspectives simultaneously!

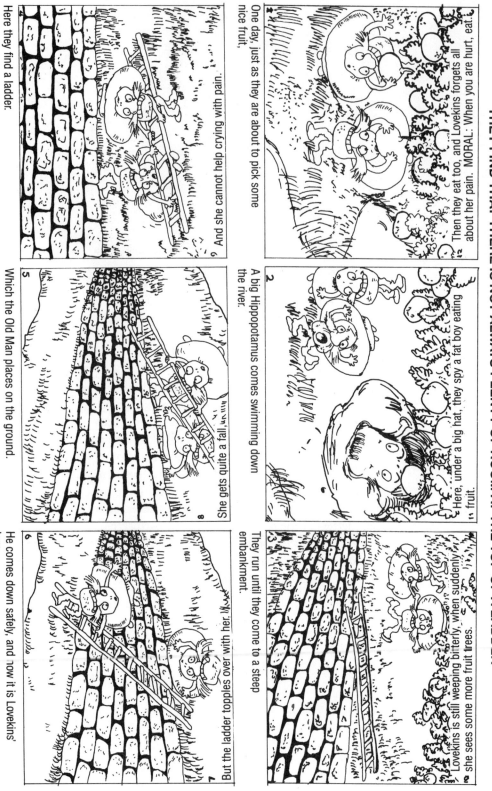

Figure 17.15

A JOLLY DAY AFTER SMALL GAME

1. Muffaroo takes a walk in the hayfields; Lovekins follows.

2. She stops to watch two dwarfs who are tossing in the hay.

3. Soon she hears a loud snoring and sees them fast asleep.

4. So she moves away softly, taking the pitchfork with her.

5. When she joins Muffaroo, he shows her a drowned owl.

6. Further on, they wade across a swiftly running stream.

7. Safe on the other shore, they go peacefully along.

8. When, suddenly, a big Owl comes swooping down on them.

9. It is the mother of the drowned owl, and she has tears in her eyes.

10. Muffaroo rushes bravely to the attack and drives the bird away.

11. After a while, they come back to the Dwarfs who are now playing and tumbling about in the hay.

12. They trot away home having had fun enough for one day.

Figure 17.16

THE BAD SNAKE AND THE GOOD WIZARD

1. Such a curious old hollow tree as they come upon one fine day. Old man Muffaroo thinks he must really have a look inside.

2. So he gayly steps into the hole, when horrors! he feels something soft and slimy and wriggly, and out he jumps again.

3. And out comes a big Snake after him, but Muffaroo, shame on him, runs away leaving poor little Lady Lovekins standing there. "How do you do," she stammers, trying to push the Snake away.

4. But the Snake will not be pushed away. He wraps himself around her instead, and pulls her into the hollow tree, where he intends to keep her captive.

5. Muffaroo, meanwhile has been running, and now he crawls, his legs having given out. He asks a squirrel if the wizard, Opnohop Moy does not live a little further on, "Yes, furders on," replies the squirrel.

6. Now the great wizard, Opnohop Moy, lives in a barrel, and all the animals and reptiles fear him. And Muffaroo arrives at his place and tells the sad tale of little Lady Lovekins' imprisonment.

7. The Wizard produces a bottle containing a magic liquer which he gives to Muffaroo saying: "Fear not the serpent more! When you meet him, call forth the name of 'Opnohop Moy' and he shall d e!"

8. The magic liquer gives Muffaroo the strength of a hundred men. "Have you seen the serpent?" he asks as he passes the squirrel again. "No serpent, sah," is the reply and the old man goes on to the tree.

9. There, the snake awaits him, and a terrible fight takes place in which Muffaroo, at first, has the better of it. But in spite of his new strength, he finds himself slowly being drawn into the hole.

10. Then suddenly, he remembers the wizard's words, and loudly he cries out the dreaded name, at which the serpent promptly rolls over and dies.

11. Dragging the dead snake out of the way, Muffaroo now helps little Lady Lovekins out of her prison.

12. And they both do a little dance to celebrate her deliverance.

Figure 17.17

More recently, the magazine *Omni* has published examples of words in which the typography has been altered to permit it to be read from more than one perspective. Thus, by turning the word upside down, the word is either the same despite the change in orientation, or it takes on a different meaning! The magazine calls such words *ambigrams*.

What does this say?

Figure 17.18 — What does this say?

Figures 17.18 and 17.19 were designed by John Langdon, of Wenonah, New Jersey. Figure 17.18 says "VICTORIA" whether you read it right-side up or upside-down. Similarly, Figure 17.19 says "AMBIGUITY" when read from either direction.

What does this say?

Figure 17.19 — What does this say?

What does this say?

Figure 17.20 – What does this say?

On the other hand, more in the manner of the cartoon by Gustave Verbeek in Figure 17.15, Robert Petrick, of New York City, designed Figure 17.20. He calls it "Tossed salad." Read one way it says "SPINACH," but when turned upside down it says "TURNIPS."

Figure 17.21 – What does this say?   **Figure 17.22 – What does this say?**

Figures 17.21, 17.22, and 17.23 appear to be written in an oriental language. They were designed by David Moser, a graduate student in Chinese at the University of Michigan. The figures are very close to Chinese characters, and can be read by a person fluent in Chinese. Such a person would read Figure 17.21 as "ENGLAND," and so can you. Just turn the book counter-clockwise 90 degrees and look at the figure!

A reader of Chinese would look at Figure 17.22 and read it as "CHINA." You can, too, if you turn the book clockwise by 90 degreees this time.

Figure 17.23 — What does this say?

Figure 17.23 could be read by either a speaker of Chinese or Japanese. They would know it says "TOKYO." Again, if you turn the book clockwise 90 degrees you can read the word—in English. These are *bilingual ambigrams!*

Figure 17.24 — What does this say?

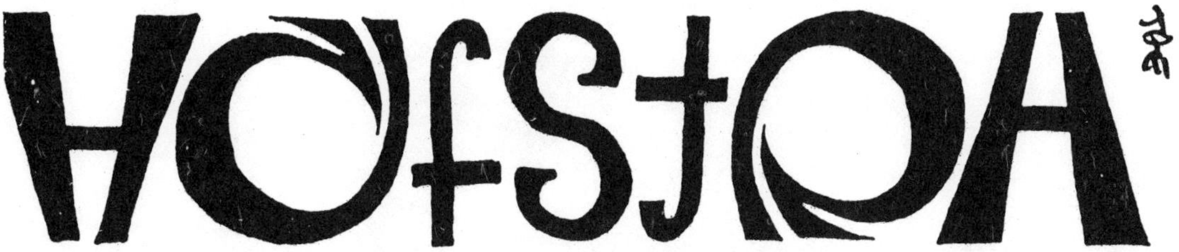

Figure 17.24 — What does this say?

You may have noticed that the authors are psychology professors at Hofstra University, in Hempstead, New York. One of our students (Jason Levy) developed the ambigram in Figure 17.22 which says HOFSTRA both ways.

You don't have to turn the book upside down to see the last visual oddities in this chapter, but you do have to turn the book.

Paul Agule

Figure 17.25 — Can you trust this man? It is written all over his face!

You can answer the question posed in Figure 17.25 if you turn the book so that the lower left-hand corner is pointing toward you. You can see clearly that he is a "liar."

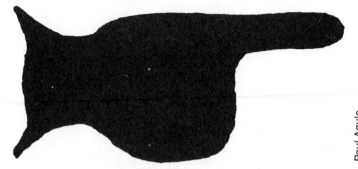

Paul Agule

Figure 17.26 — Giving directions, or a cat?

Notice the difference in the meaning of Figure 17.26 when you turn the book 90 degrees clockwise. The same figure, when seen in this perspective, is interpreted very differently.

Figure 17.27 — Just a clown, or the whole circus?

Finally, artist Larry Kettlekamp of Cranbury, New Jersey, designed Figure 17.27. With the book held in its normal position, you can clearly see a clown's face. Turning it clockwise 90 degrees, you can see the whole circus! (From Kettlekamp, 1974)

CHAPTER

TWO EYES ARE BETTER THAN ONE

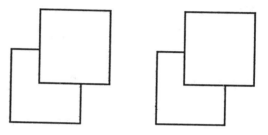

We are not always aware that we have two eyes, each seeing a slightly different picture of the world because they are not in the same point in space. This was not recognized scientifically until 1838 when Sir Charles Wheatstone presented a paper to the Royal Society in England, in which he connected our ability to see three dimensions with the fact that we have two eyes seeing the world from different perspectives. Sir Wheatstone invented the *stereoscope* that year. The stereoscope presents slightly different pictures of the same object to each eye. Two pictures are taken of an object with two cameras mounted alongside one another and positioned the same distance apart as a pair of eyes would be. The stereoscope shows each eye only one picture, resulting in what is called *retinal disparity*. The brain is able to blend them into a single image. The result is referred to as *binocular vision.*

You can demonstrate that each eye "takes a different picture" by holding one finger in front of you and alternately opening and closing each eye. Your finger will appear to move back and forth.

The brain is extremely sensitive to very small differences in pictures sent to each eye. In fact, it is so sensitive that the stereoscope can be used in examining possible counterfeit bills, and in ballistics testing. When this is done, a bill known to be genuine is viewed with one eye, while a suspect bill is viewed with the other with a stereoscope. Even minute differences are quickly detected. Similarly, if you view markings on a bullet fired from a specific gun, and compare it to another bullet, since no two guns make exactly the same marks, you cannot match up those fired from different guns, but you can if they are fired from the same gun.

Most of the figures in this chapter consist of pairs which can be combined to form a single image. To do this, place a piece of cardboard on edge between the two figures, perpendicular to the book. Then position your face so that your left eye sees only the left figure and your right eye only the right figure. Allow the two images to merge by gently crossing your eyes.

You can also merge the two pictures by simply crossing your eyes. Using a pencil point to focus upon may help. Place the pencil about half way from your eyes to the figure and focus on the point. Your eyes will cross about the correct amount. Gradually try not to pay attention to the pencil, but rather the figures beyond it. At some point, the two figures will seem to "pop" into focus and fuse together. Once this happens, you can remove the pencil and stare at the figure. With practice, you can become quite good at fusing such pictures even without the use of a pencil. It is important that the book be held level so that the images merge evenly.

In the 1950's, 3-D movies were briefly popular. In this case, two images were presented with some degree of overlap. Again, the images represented the different views for each eye. One image was red and the other was green. Each image was presented to a different eye by having special glasses with one green filter and one red filter. The red object could not be seen through the red filter, nor the green object through the green filter. The brain took these two separate pictures and fused them into a three-dimensional image.

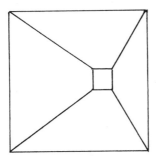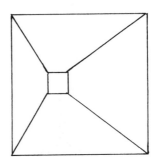

Figure 18.1 — A pyramid.

In Figures 18.1 and 18.2, the fused image will be
a three-dimensional object. Figure 18.1 will have a
pyramidal shape, and 18.2 will appear to be a crystal.

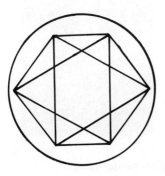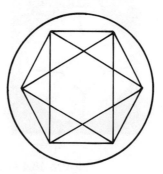

Figure 18.2 — A crystal.

Figure 18.3 does not become three dimensional, but rather, when each eye is shown a different picture (one eye seeing only the cage and the other eye only the bird). If you cross your eyes slightly, the two are blended, and the bird seems to be in the cage.

Figure 18.3 — Can you put the bird in the cage?

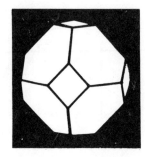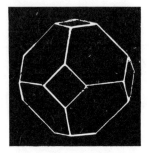

Figure 18.4 — Binocular translucence.

Yet a different binocular effect is seen in Figure 18.4. Since one of the figures is black and the other white, if each one is presented to a different eye at the same time, the brain will take the two different colors and make the figure appear translucent.

In the chapter on Depth Perception we noted that if an object appears to cover another, it is assumed to be closer to us. In Figure 18.5, a complete square appears to be covering another square which we assume to be further away. Note that we tend to assume the second figure is a square. It obviously could be an inverted "L-shaped" figure on the same plane as the square, but with shared edges.

If you allow your eyes to cross gently so that the two images fuse into one, the L-shaped figure actually appears to be in front of the square! (Kaufman, 1974)

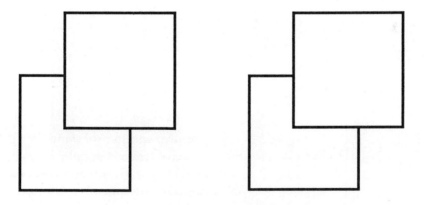

Figure 18.5 — Which figure is on top?

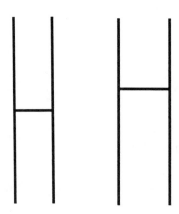

Figure 18.6 —

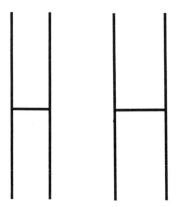

Figure 18.7 —

Figure 18.8 —

Figures 18.6 and 18.7 show interesting differences when perceived stereoscopically. In each case, there are parallel lines which are connected by a horizontal line. The left-hand figure of each is slightly narrower than the right-hand figure. In Figure 18.6 the horizontal line is at the same level, while in Figure 18.7 it is at a different level. Apparently the brain has difficulty with this difference! Figure 18.6 when viewed stereoscopically is simply an "H-shaped" figure. On the other hand, Figure 18.7 is never quite fused and appears to have three vertical and two horizontal lines as shown in Figure 18.8! (James, 1908)

Figure 18.9 — Can you see three lines?

Figure 18.9 also involves binocular vision, but you do not have to view it stereoscopically. The figure appears to be two straight lines which cross. You can "create" a third line at their intersection which looks like a short pin sticking up through the paper! To see this you must tilt the book away from you so that it is almost perpendicular to your eyes. Hold it so that the cross point is directly in front of you. If you cross your eyes slightly to focus on the cross point, you will see the third line! This illusion was first reported in the classic text *Principles of Psychology* by William James in 1980. He attributed it to a psychologist named Christine Ladd Franklin who was the first woman president of the American Psychological Association. (James, 1908).

C H A P T E R 19

OTHER ILLUSIONS

If a straight line disappears at an angle behind a solid surface, and reappears at the other side, it will seem to be in the "wrong" place to most people. This is referred to as *Poggendorf's illusion*. You can demonstrate for yourself by drawing a straight line at least twelve inches long at about a 45 degree angle. If you place this book across the line so that part of the line is on either side of the book, the line will not appear to be continuous.

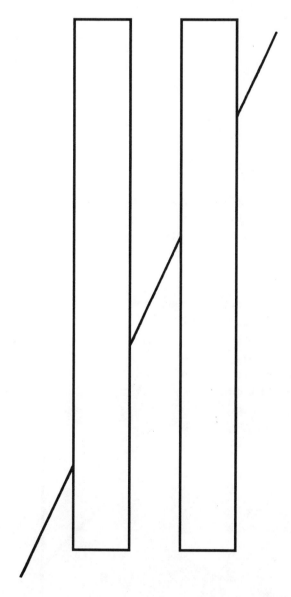

Figure 19.1 – Is there one diagonal line or three?

Figures 19.1, 19.2, and 19.3 are all examples of *Poggendorf's illusion.* In Figure 19.1, the diagonal lines that are interrupted by the rectangles appear to be three separate lines. In fact, placing a straight edge against the line will demonstrate that they are segments of one straight line.

Figure 19.2 — Does A or B continue to C?

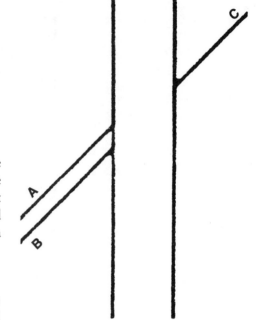

Figure 19.2 is a variation of 19.1. In this case we have placed a second diagonal line parallel to the first. It has been drawn to represent what most people see as a continuous line; even though "A" and "C" belong together, line "B" appears to continue on as "C."

Again, in Figure 19.3, when the vertical lines interrupt the diagonal, most people believe "B" will touch "A" below where "A" intersects the parallel lines, while in actuality, the two lines meet. When it is inverted and tilted, the short line is more likely to appear to correctly intersect at the bottom of "A." These are examples of *Poggendorf's illusion.*

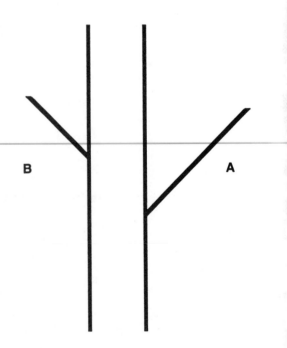

Figure 19.3 — Where do lines A & B meet?

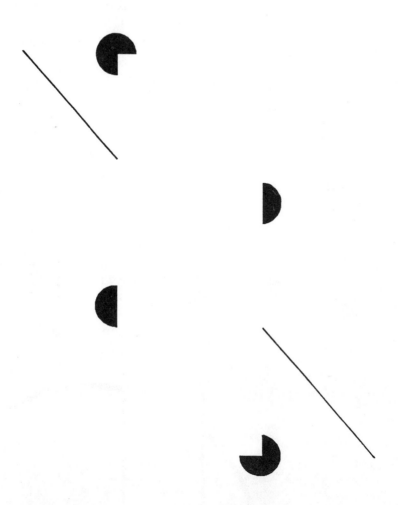

Figure 19.4 – A variation of Poggendorf's illusion.

The strength of Poggendorf's illusion is shown in Figures 19.4 and 19.5. Figure 19.4 shows that Poggendorf's illusion works even when the intervening figure is an illusory figure of the kind discussed in Chapter 5 (Fineman, 1981).

Figure 19.5 – A variation of Poggendorf's illusion.

Figure 19.5 shows that it does not even require solid lines. In Figure 19.5 most people do not think that the four dots which go from the upper left to the lower right are on a straight line (Coren, 1970).

You do not have to have a straight line apparently passing through an area to demonstrate the Poggendorf illusion. In Figure 19.6, what appears to be a circle is interrupted by a pair of parallel lines. However, the curved lines which make up the circle do not appear to be continuous. The left curved section appears to be slightly smaller than the larger one.

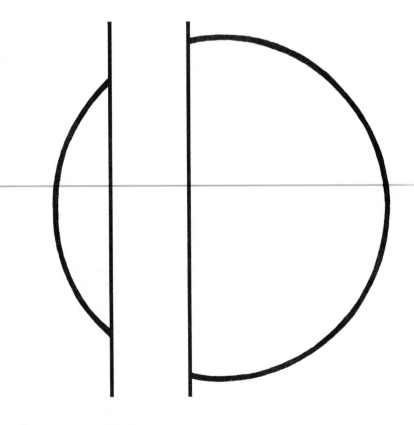

Figure 19.6 – A variation of Poggendorf's illusion.

Figure 19.7 — Distortion in viewing through a different medium.

The straw in the water glass in Figure 19.7 does not appear to continue in a straight line, but this is not an example of Poggendorf's illusion. It is the result of light being "bent" by water which is a thicker medium than air. If you were to literally shoot fish in a barrel, you would have to adjust your aim to compensate for this phenomenon. The fish would not be where they appeared to be in looking down through the water.

Figures 19.8, 19.9, and 19.10 are examples of visual vibration. The patterns of alternating light and dark areas strike different parts of the retina as the eye makes its natural movements, and cause a "flashing" sensation. This effect, often used in Optical Art, is similar to the moire pattern seen in some silk materials. The effect is exaggerated if the illustrations are moved slightly.

Figure 19.8 — Visual vibration.

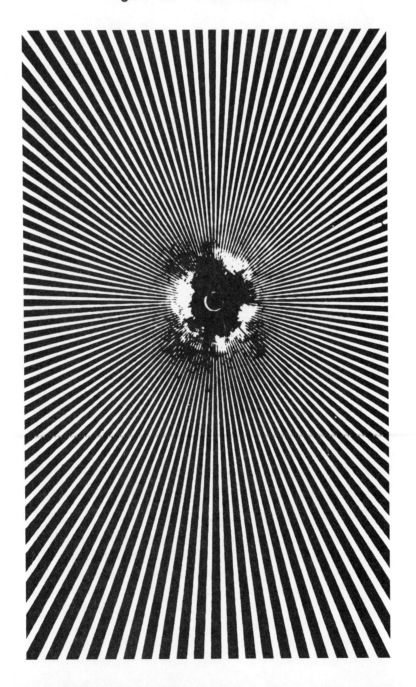

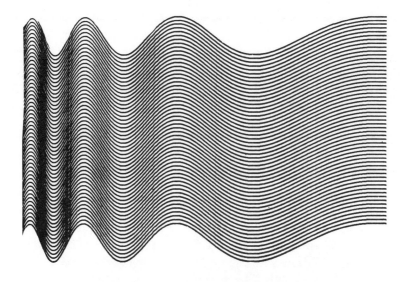

Figure 19.9 — Visual vibration.

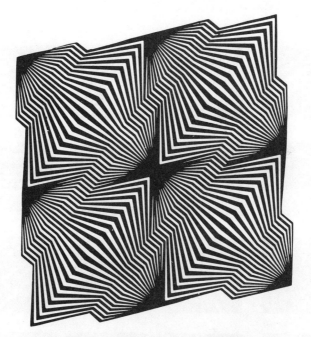

Figure 19.10 — Visual vibrations.

There is still another interesting aftereffect which can be seen when using images which produce "visual vibration." If you stare at Figures 19.8, 19.9 or 19.10 for about 30 seconds (to produce an aftereffect) the visual sensation is one of streaming movement. It has been described as moving grains of rice. The direction of the streaming is at right angles to the main lines of the figure (Robinson, 1972).

Figure 19.11 — Can you make the face disappear?

Each eye has a *blind spot* where nerves leave the eye and go to the brain. There are no light receptors at this spot. To find your blind spot, close your left eye and fixate your right eye on the target at the left in Figure 19.11. The face will disappear because the light reflected from it will be falling on your blind spot.

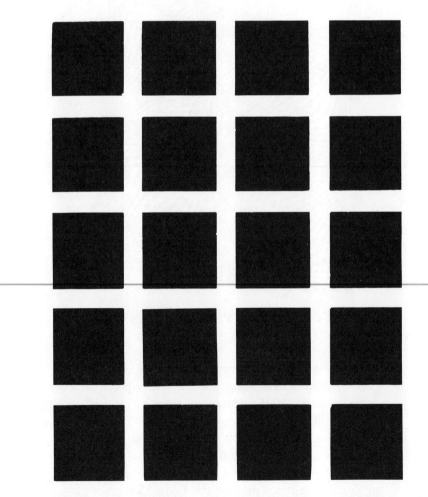

Figure 19.12 — Are there gray spots at the intersections?

Small gray spots can be seen at the intersections of the squares in Figure 19.12, but if you look directly at any one intersection, the gray spot disappears! The same illusion is achieved if the squares are white, as in Figure 19.13. This illusion is known as *Hermann's grid.*

Figure 19.13 — Are there gray spots at the intersections?

A variation of Hermann's grid may be seen in Figure 19.14. If you fix your gaze on the figure, it may appear that the printing of the illustration was not particularly clean. That is, small pinpoints of "dirt" seem to be in many of the small white squares. As with Hermann's grid, if you shift your gaze to any individual white square, or allow your eyes to move about the figure, all of the white squares are perfectly "clean."

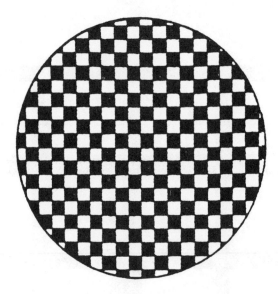

Figure 19.14 — Did the printer leave pinpoints of dots in some of the white squares?

Your eye has a small hole through which light passes—the *pupil*. The back wall is where the *retina* is located—the part of the eye which picks up light waves. It is important to remember that this surface is not flat. It means that different parts of the *retina* are at different distances from the *pupil*. While we are not usually aware of this, it plays a part in what we see.

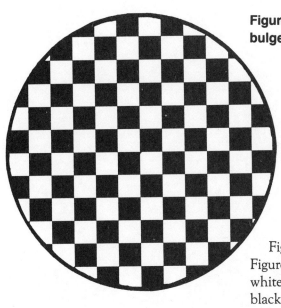

Figure 19.15 — This looks flat, but can be made to bulge outward

Figures 19.15 and 19.16 look like checkerboards. Figure 19.15 appears to have equal size black and white squares. In Figure 19.16, only the very center black and white areas look square. However, if you look at Figure 19.15 by placing the book about an inch from one of your eyes, it will appear to bulge out toward you in a ball-like shape. On the other hand, viewing Figure 19.16 from about an inch away makes the black and white areas seem much more regular in shape and flatter than it looks from a distance.

These shapes change because the *retina* is curved. We usually view things from a great enough distance that only a part of the *retina* is involved. In addition, we tend to concentrate on the image in the center of our field of vision, rather than at the edges. When you fill up the field of vision by looking at these figures from only an inch away, the entire *retina* is stimulated approximately equally.

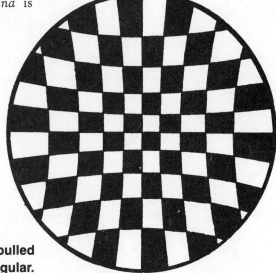

Figure 19.16 — This looks like it is being pulled outward, but can be made to be flat and regular.

CHAPTER 20

EPILOGUE

The title of this book is *Can You Believe Your Eyes?* We hope by now you know the answer is—not always. There are many conditions under which what you see is not an accurate representation of what exists. This is not only true for human beings, but is occasionally true for animals as well.

Birds do not usually respond to a painted image of another bird. Under certain conditions, however, the behavior of birds can be altered by painted images of other birds.

In 1988, the New York newspaper *Newsday*, published an article about a problem the New York Port Authority was having with sea gulls. It seems that the sea gulls were cracking open shell fish by dropping them on an airport area used by helicopters. Once the shell was open, the birds would swoop down to eat the food. This was creating a dangerous situation with birds flying into the helicopters. The helicopters, and passengers as well, would sometimes slip on the combination of broken shells and left over debris. The solution was found in painting images of flying gulls on the landing pad.

It was interesting that the painted birds only stopped the real ones from dropping the shells when all of the images were painted as flying in the same direction. The first time the birds were painted on the pad, they appeared to be flying in a variety of directions. This pattern did not stop the live gulls from dropping shells. However, when the silhouettes of the birds were painted as all flying in the same direction, as though gliding with the wind, the real birds no longer used the concrete pad to break the shells.

Apparently when gulls fly in a variety of directions they are not usually interested in feeding. When they glide with the wind, they are usually either looking for food or a place to drop a shell. Presumably the real birds feared the painted birds were hunting for food and would steal shells which were dropped. The real birds believed their eyes!

This book has presented hundreds of ways in which your eyes have been similarly fooled. The overwhelming number of examples have involved what are largely external influences on perception. That is, although the brain interprets the visual stimulus incorrectly, since the error in judgment is nearly universal, it is less the characteristics of the individual than the stimulus and context.

But perceptions are influenced and distorted by internal factors as well. Your senses can be "fooled" by your ideas and your wishes every bit as much as by the information your eyes receive from the outside. People often see what they expect to see. If you are waiting for a friend who is late for an appointment, and you see a person some distance away moving toward you, you may be able to recognize him at a far greater distance than usual. If you are prepared to see him you can respond more quickly to cues than would otherwise be the case.

However, it is also possible to be very embarrassed if you start to wave wildly, only to find out the person is a total stranger. When you are set to see something you want to see you may overreact incorrectly to minor similarities between the distant person you actually see and the one you are eager to see.

At the opposite extreme, you may momentarily not recognize a person you know extremely well, if you are in a place or situation in which you would definitely not expect to see the person.

Our point is that you cannot always believe your senses. They can fool you, at least some of the time. Sometimes the source of the distortion is largely in the objects themselves, and the context in which they are seen. Under certain conditions, as we have seen throughout the book, there are common if not universal misperceptions by both humans and animals. Sometimes with people, the distortion is a result of individual characteristics—one's attitudes, motivations, or expectations. These are highly individual. Nonetheless, when these factors operate, one often sees what one wants to see, and what fits in with preconceptions.

It can be argued that perception often is a poor representation of reality. Yet it is important to recognize that a person's behavior is controlled less by what is actually true, than what the person believes is true. Perceptions may be more important than reality in determining behavior!

REFERENCES

Ames, Jr., A. (1951). Visual perception and the rotating trapezoidal window. *Psychological Monographs, 65,* No. 324.

Atkinson, R.L., Atkinson, R.C., Smith, E.E. and Hilgard, E.R., (1987). *Introduction to Psychology: 9th ed.* Harcourt Brace.

Benjamin, Jr., L.T., Hopkins, J.R. and Nation, J.R. (1987). *Psychology.* Macmillan Publishing Co.

Blakemore, C. and Sutton, P. (1969). Size adaptation: A new aftereffect. *Science, 166,* 245–247.

Botwinick, J. (1961). Husband and father-in-law: A reversible figure. *American Journal of Psychology, 74,* 312–313.

Bradley, D.R. and Dumais, S.R. (1975). Ambiguous cognitive contours. *Nature, 257,* 582–584.

Bradley, D.R., and Petry, H.M. (1977). Organizational determinants of subjective contour. *American Journal of Psychology, 90,* 253–262.

Bugelski, B.R. and Alampay, D.A. (1961). The role of frequency in developing perceptual sets. *Canadian Journal of Psychology, 15,* 205–211.

Charmichael, L. (1951). Another "hidden figure" picture. *American Journal of Psychology, 64,* 137–138.

Coren, S. (1970). Lateral inhibition and the Wundt-Hering illusion. *Psychonomic Science, 18,* 341–342.

Coren, S. (1972). Subjective contour and apparent depth. *Psychological Review, 79,* 359–367.

Coren, S. & Girgus, J.S. (1978). *Seeing is Deceiving: The Psychology of Visual Illusions,* Lawrence Erlbaum Associates, Hillsdale, N.J.

Coren, S. & Miller, J. (1974). Size contrast as a function of figural similarity. *Perception and Psychophysics, 16,* 355–357.

Dallenbach, K.M. (1951). A puzzle-picture with a new principle of concealment. *American Journal of Psychology, 64,* 431–433.

Draper, S.W. (1978). The Penrose triangle and a family of related figures. *Perception*, 7, 283–296.

Ebbinghaus, H. (1902). *Grundzuege der Psycholgie*, Vols. I & II. Leipzig: Viet.

Ehrenstein, W. (1925). Versuche uber die Bezuehungen zwichen Bewegungs und Gestaltwahrnehmung. *Z. Psychol.*, 95, 305–352.

Erb, M.B. and Dallenback, K.M. (1939). Subjective colors from line patterns. *American J. Psychology*, 52, 227–241.

Fechner, G.T. (1838). Ueber Scheiben zur Darstellung subjectiver Farben, *Pogg. Ann. d. Physik u. Chemie*. 121, 227–232.

Fineman, M. (1981). *The Inquisitive Eye*. Oxford University Press.

Fisher, G.H. (1967a). Measuring ambiguity. *American Journal of Psychology*, 80, 541–557.

Fisher, G.H. (1967b). Preparation of ambiguous stimulus materials. *Perception and Psychophysics*, 2, 421–422.

Fisher, G.H. (1968a). Ambiguity of form: Old and new. *Perception and Psychophysics*, 4, 189–192.

Fisher, G.H. (1968b). 'Mother, father and daughter': A three-aspect ambiguous figure. *American Journal of Psychology*, 81, 274–277.

Fraser, J. (1908). A new illusion of direction. *British J. of Psychology*, 2, 307–320.

Frisby, J.P. (1980). *Seeing, Illusion, Brain and Mind*. Oxford University Press.

Frisby, J.P. and Clatworthy, J.L. (1975). Illusory contours: curious cases of simultaneous brightness contrast? *Perception*, 4, 349–357.

Gardner, M. (1970). Of optical illusions, from figures that are undetectable to hot dogs that float. *Scientific American*, 222, May, 124–127.

Gregory, R.L. (1970). *The Intelligent Eye*. McGraw-Hill.

Hanson, N.R. (1958). *Patterns of Discovery*. Cambridge University Press.

Hill, W.E. (1915). My wife and my mother-in-law. *Puck*, November 6th, 11.

Huffman, D.A. (1971). Impossible objects as nonsense sentences. In *Machine Intelligence 6*. Eds B. Meltzer, D. Michie (Edinburgh: Edinburgh University Press), 295–323.

James, W. (1908). *Principles of Psychology – Volume II*. Henry Holt.

Judd, C.H. (1899). A study of geometrical illusions. *Psychological Review*, 6, 241–261.

Kanisza, G. (1976). Subjective contours. *Scientific American*, 234, April, 48–52.

Kaufman, L. (1974). *Sight and Mind: An Introduction to visual perception*. Oxford University Press.

Kennedy, J.M. (1976). Sun figure: an illusory diffuse contour resulting from an arrangement of dots. *Perception, 5,* 480–481.

Kettelkamp, L. (1974). *Tricks of Eye and Mind: The Story of Optical Illusions.* William Morrow & Co., N.Y.

Kohler, W. & Wallach, H. (1944). Figural aftereffects: an investigation of visual processes. *Proceedings of the American Philosophical Society,* 88, 269–357.

Kolers, P.A. (1964). The boys from Syracuse: Another ambiguous figure. *American Journal of Psychology, 77,* 671–672.

Leeman, F., Effers, J. and Schuyt, M. (1976). *Hidden Images: Games of Perception, Anamorphic Art, Illusion.* Harry N. Abrams, Inc. New York.

Leeper, R. (1935). A study of a neglected portion of the field of learning: The development of sensory organization. *Journal of Genetic Psychology, 46,* 41–75.

Luckiesh, M. (1965). *Visual Illusions: Their Causes, Characteristics and Applications.* Dover Publications.

MacKay, D.M. (1957). Moving images produced by regular stationary patterns. *Nature, 180,* 849–850.

Obonai, T. (1954). Induction effects in estimates of extent. *J. Experimental Psychology, 47,* 57–60.

Orbison, W.D. (1939). Shape as a function of the vector field. *American Journal of Psychology.* 52, 31–45.

Osgood, C.E. (1953). *Method and Theory in Experimental Psychology,* New York: Oxford University Press.

Oyama, T. (1960). Japanese studies in the so-called geometrical optical illusions. *Psychologia, 3,* 7–20.

Parks, T.E. (1984). Illusory figures: A (mostly) atheoretical review. *Psychological Bulletin, 95,* 282–300.

Parks, T.E. and Coss, R.G. (1986). Prime illusion. *Psychology Today,* October, 6–9.

Penrose, L.S. and Penrose, R. (1958). Impossible objects: A special type of visual illusion *British Journal of Psychology, 49,* 31–33.

Perkins, D.N. (1976). How good a bet is good form? *Perception, 5,* 393–406.

Petry, S.J. (1975). *A combination of perceptual and sensitivity changes occurring during metacontrast masking.* Dissertation Abstracts International. 35, 3622b.

Psychological Corporation. (1955). *The Multi-aptitude Test: Form B,* The Psychological Corporation.

Ramachandran, V.S. (1988). Perceiving Shape from Shading. *Scientific American*, August, 259, 2, 76–83.

Richardson, R.I. (1979). The nonequivalence of abrupt and diffuse illusory contours. *Perception*, 8, 589–593.

Robinson, J.O. (1972). *The Psychology of Visual Illusion*. London, Hutchinson University Library.

Ruch, F.L. (1967). *Psychology and Life, 7th ed*. Scott, Foresman.

Schuster, D.H. (1964). A new ambiguous figure: A three-stick clevis. *American J. of Psychology*, 77, 673.

Simon, C. (1987). Place maps. *Psychology Today*, November, 15.

Skinner, B.F. (1932). A paradoxical color effect. *J. General Psychology*, 7, 481–482.

Street, R.F. (1931). *A Gestalt Completion Test*. New York: Bureau of Publications, Teachers College, Columbia University.

Traylor, T. (1965). Nuns and nudes. In R. Prelisser, Vision in engineering. *International Science and Technology*, 46, 61–66.

Wade, N. (1982). *The art and science of visual illusions*. Routledge & Kegan Paul, London.

Walker, J. (1988). The Amature Scientist. *Scientific American*. January, 96–100.

Wertheimer, M. (1912). Experimentelle Studien uber das Schen von Bewegung. *Z. Psychologe*, 61, 161–265.

Wundt, W. (1898). Die geometrisch-optischen Tauschungen. *Abhandl. mathphyis. ser sachs. Ges. Wiss.*, 24, 53–178.

COPYRIGHT ACKNOWLEDGMENTS

The authors and publishers thank the owners of copyright materials (listed below) for permission to use them in this work. In the event there is any discrepancy regarding permission for materials or their use, the publishers will rectify any such errors, when the book is reprinted, upon written request from the copyright owners.

2.4–2.6   From "Ambiguity of form: Old and new" by G.H. Fisher, 1968, *Perception and Psychophysics, 4,* 189–192. Copyright 1968 by Psychonomic Society, Inc., Reprinted by permission.

2.8   "Husband and father-in-law: Reversible figure" by J. Botwinick, 1961, *American Journal of Psychology, 74,* 312–313. Copyright 1961 University of Illinois Press. Reprinted by permission.

2.9   "Mother, father and daughter: A three aspect ambiguous figure" by G.H. Fisher, 1968, *American Journal of Psychology, 81,* 274–277. Copyright 1968 by University of Illinois Press. Reprinted by permission.

2.10   From Bugelski, B.R. and Alampay, D.A. (1961) "The role of frequency in developing sets." *Canadian Journal of Psychology, 15,* 205–211. Copyright 1961 Canadian Psychological Association. Reprinted with permission.

2.11   From "Preparation of ambiguous stimulus materials" by G.H. Fisher, 1967, *Perception and Psychophysics, 2,* 421–422. Reprinted with permission from the Psychonomic Society, Inc., and the author.

2.12   Reprinted with permission of Macmillan Publishing Company. From *Psychology* by J.R. Nation, L.T. Benjamin and J.R. Hopkins. Copyright 1987 Macmillan Publishing Company.

2.13   "Measuring and Ambiguity" by G.H. Fisher, 1967, *American Journal of Psychology, 80,* 541–557. Copyright 1967 University of Illinois Press. Reprinted by permission.

2.14   From Hanson, N.R. (1958) *Patterns of Discovery,* Cambridge University Press. Reprinted by permission.

2.15   Copyright Al Hirschfeld. Drawing reproduced by special arrangement with Hirschfeld's exclusive representative, the Margo Feiden Galleries, New York.

8.3, 8.4, 8.5, 8.6, 8.7, 8.14 From "Penrose family and family of related pictures" by S.W. Draper, 1978, *Perception*, 7, 283–296. Reprinted by permission.

8.9 From "A new ambiguous figure: a three-stick clevis" by D.H. Schuster, 1977, *American Journal of Psychology*, 77, 673. Copyright 1977 University of Illinois Press. Reprinted by permission.

8.10 From Roger Hayward, *Mathematical Games* by Martin Gardner, p. 124. Copyright 1970. *Scientific American*. Reprinted by permission

8.15 "How good a bet is good form?" by D.N. Perkins, 1976, *Perception*, 5, 393–406. Copyright 1976, *Perception*. Reprinted by permission.

8.8, 8.16–8.24 inclusive From "impossible objects as nonsense sentences" by D.A. Huffman, 1971, *Machine Intelligence*. Copyright 1971 by Edinburgh University Press. Reprinted by permission.

9.8 Reprinted with permission from *Vision Research*, 14, 1421–1432, Klein, S., Stromeyer, III, C.F., and Ganz, L. "The simultaneous spatial frequency shift: a dissociation between the detection and perception of gratings." Copyright 1974, Pergamon Press plc.

10.6 From "Japanese studies in so-called geometrical optical illustrations" by T. Olyama, 1960, *Psychologia*, 3, 7–20. Copyright 1960 by *Psychologia*. Reprinted by permission.

11.8 Reprinted by permission of the Jefferson National Expansion Memorial/NPS.

12.11 From "Illusory contours: curious cases of simultaneous brightness contrast" by J.P. Frisby and J.L. Clatworthy, 1975, *Perception*, 4, 349–357. Reprinted by permission of the publisher and the author.

13.7 From "Subjective contour and apparent depth" by S. Coren, 1972, *Psychological Review*, 79, 359–367. Copyright 1972 by American Psychological Association. Reprinted by permission of the author.

14.1–14.12 inclusive Courtesy of Paul Agule.

15.5 From *Method and Theory in Experimental Psychology* by Charles E. Osgood. Copyright 1953 by Oxford University Press, Inc.: renewed 1981 by Charles E. Osgood. Reprinted by permission.

15.7, 15.8, 15.9 *Journal of Genetic Psychology*, 46, 41–75, 1935. Reprinted with permission of the Helen Dwight Reid Educational Foundation. Published by Heldref Publications, 40000 Albemarle St. NW Washington, DC, 20016. Copyright 1935.

15.10 From *The Multi-aptitude Test: Form B* by Edward and Louise Cureton, 1955. The Psychological Corporation, San Antonio, TX.

16.1 Copyright 1960 by The New York Times Company. Reprinted by permission. Photograph reprinted by permission of Joseph Raftery, Miami, FL.

16.2 From "CDC paints a picture of HIV infection in US" by William Booth, 1988, *Science*, 239, 253. Copyright 1988 by the AAAS. Reprinted by permission.

OTHER WORKS BY THE AUTHORS

Professors Yuker and Block have developed other materials which entertain and educate. Among them are several decks of conventional playing cards (52 cards and 4 suits), which have unusual faces. The faces convey interesting information, yet at the same time, permit playing such card games as bridge or poker within the regular rules for such games. Two of these decks feature many of the illusions contained in this book as well as a sixteen page booklet for each deck.

A third deck is called *The Graduates*. In this deck, the Kings, Queens and Jacks wear academic robes representing 24 different doctoral degrees and 24 universities. This deck includes an eight page booklet describing the history of academic gowns and the color code for the doctoral hoods representing the various degrees.

They have also issued the first two in a series of Map Decks. These highly unusual cards depict complete maps of Central London and Manhattan respectively, and are printed in full color. Each includes a booklet listing all major streets and places of interest in each city. Thus, for example, Trafalgar Square can be found on the two of Hearts in the London Map Deck, while the Empire State Building is on the King of Diamonds in the New York Map Deck. The cards can be used as a map, and also to play card games such as bridge or poker. Other major cities are planned to follow in this series.

For information about any of these products contact:

Y & B Associates Inc.
33 Primrose Lane
Hempstead, N.Y.
11550
FAX (516) 481-0256

Y & B Associates Inc.
Products that Entertain and Educate.